FLEW by the SEAT of my PANTS

ART FRANKEL

iUniverse, Inc.
Bloomington

Flew by the Seat of My Pants

iUniverse books may be ordered through booksellers or by contacting:

iUniverse
1663 Liberty Drive
Bloomington, IN 47403
www.iuniverse.com
1-800-Authors (1-800-288-4677)

ISBN: 978-1-4502-6927-8 (pbk)
ISBN: 978-1-4502-6929-2 (cloth)
ISBN: 978-1-4502-6928-5 (ebk)

Printed in the United States of America

iUniverse rev. date: 12/22/10

Dedication

I dedicate this book to my beautiful wife, Shirley. A man can achieve almost anything with a woman like her. She has always been understanding, tolerant, forgiving, and loving. She did not always agree with everything I did, but she always supported me. I'd also like to dedicate this book to my great family.

Acknowledgments

I would like to thank my friend Bob Burris for his expertise and hard work. This book would not have been possible without him. I would also like to thank my grandson Jesse Frankel for his creativity designing the cover. Also thanks to Krista Hill, Brian Rouff, and Jim Boeke for their contributions.

Introduction

What makes someone extraordinary? You have scientists who make great discoveries in space; doctors who develop new cures for cancer and other fatal diseases; people who invent devices that make life easier, more pleasant, and safer; politicians who rise to the top in government; and astronauts who risk their lives in space. Most of us are like me: an ordinary person, average intelligence, married with a family who plugs along every day to survive. Sounds boring, doesn't it? Well, it doesn't have to be.

I was and still am an ordinary person, born in the Bronx and raised on a farm in Connecticut. I survived the Great Depression and World War II, all while tolerating anti-Semitic behavior from people in high school and in town. I went into the military, then to college, got married, started a family, worked too many jobs and occupations to mention or remember, always learning something new. I ended up with a career in education, traveled in Europe and the U.S. with groups and my family by plane, train, automobile, boat, and foot. I built my own boat and sailed it all the way to Hawaii and back. I left education when state funding was greatly reduced and eventually became an actor. I have been blessed with five great kids, ten grandkids, and three great-grandkids — so far.

I live up in the San Bernardino mountains in Lake Arrowhead, which I love. I still drive to Hollywood for acting auditions. I have yet to be nominated for an Emmy or an Oscar, but I do get a job every once in a while. In my spare time I read and watch TV with my wife. I'm looking for a new hobby. I'm eighty-one and still having fun.

Life is precious, life is a journey, and you should enjoy the ride. I know it's been said before and it may sound corny, but I don't care; I've been there. If you have dreams, pick the best one and go for it; give it a shot. You might surprise the hell out of yourself.

If your present career starts to sour or you get tired of your job, start to train for something else, something you love to do. Everybody is multi-talented. Who says there is only one job that you should do for the rest of your life? People are living longer today, and with technology advancing at such a rapid pace, new careers are popping up all the time. Never plan to retire; just keep changing careers. Remember to pick something you love to do, something that you can do for the rest of your life.

As I look back on my life, it seems as though a common thread ran through it: I took all kinds of risks and chances without giving some of them a great deal of thought. I flew by the seat of my pants, like the old World War I Lafayette Escadrille fighter pilots used to say, but it always seemed to work out.

I must admit I've had a very unfair advantage; I had, and still have, the greatest woman companion a man could have. I didn't know anything about her, except that she was adopted, and had no family background of any kind. She was adopted from the Tennessee Children's Home Society, which turned out to be the most scandalous, abusive, illegal agency in the history of the U.S. Again, I lucked out with a great lady. My Hebrew name is "Avraham" or Abraham, םָרְבַא in Hebrew. Shirley's original name is Sarah or שׂ ָרָה in Hebrew. Abraham and Sarah were husband and wife in the Old Testament. It seems as if we were destined to be together.

I've managed to learn quite a few lessons in eighty years. It is my most sincere wish that some of what I have to share with you will help make your life even just a little bit better. You don't have to have done anything extraordinary as long as your wife and kids and friends who love you think you're extraordinary. That's what matters.

Art Frankel, January 2010

Chapter One

When you're tempted to think of something as being bad luck, you might just be wrong.

On the morning of October 22, 2007, a one-hundred-foot wall of flames hot enough to melt metal raced through the idyllic mountain community of Lake Arrowhead, California. Pine trees exploded in the fierce heat, firefighters bravely assaulted the flames, risking their lives to save the homes lying in the inferno's path. Despite their efforts, over 176 houses were reduced to ash and rubble. One of them was the dream house that Shirley, my wife of sixty years, and I had designed and built ourselves ten years earlier.

We officially moved in during June of 1997, just Shirley, me, and our three dogs, Sadie, Sydney, and Stimpy. It was a beautiful mountain escape, with views of pine-covered mountains, desert peaks, and Mt. San Gorgonio at 11,499 feet tall, the highest mountain in southern California. In 2003, my grown daughter Rochelle moved in with us and brought a little Chihuahua with her. Shirley liked the dog so much, we bought another one. Over the next few years we added four cats, a blue-tick coon hound, a pit bull, you name it; our house was practically a kennel. 2400 square feet with four bedrooms, three baths, cool in the summer and warm in the winter, thanks to our wood-burning stove in the living room. We had a deck on the main floor where we could take in the views, enjoy the breeze, and feed the birds. We put in a second deck down below and a two-car garage. It was a very, very comfortable house and we loved it. And then one morning the wind screamed, blew down an Edison pole, and

1

started a fire. The sheriff ordered us to evacuate or possibly lose our lives, and everything changed.

I will never forget the day — after the fires had been contained — that we returned to see what was left of our home. Coming up the mountain was fine, but when we could actually see where the fire had been, everything was so completely devastated it looked like an atomic bomb had gone off. Everything was flattened; the ground barren and gray and scorched. It wasn't as if there'd been a fire and a few minor structures had burned, or perhaps the corner of a house was still there — almost everything was completely leveled. Black sticks protruded from the ashen soil — trunks of trees that had been charred. Incredibly, every so often a house right in the middle of the devastation was still standing, completely untouched by the flames.

As we pulled up to what had been our home just several days earlier, only the driveway was left. It was as if our home had never even existed. The wind, I was told later, had accelerated to over one hundred miles per hour coming up the hill. The wind was so fierce and it made the fire so hot that it melted things you wouldn't have thought possible. The burned skeletons of cars sat in the road, their alloy wheels liquified. We got out of the car and slowly walked down our driveway to assess the damage. The raging flames were so hot that they actually destroyed the concrete, popping the concrete out of the driveway.

We looked down below at all of the debris; some of our appliances were so twisted that we couldn't tell what they originally had been. I couldn't even recognize my snow blower.

At that moment, seeing that literally nothing was left of the house we'd worked all of our lives for, it was impossible to envision what would happen next. What I didn't realize is that what seemed like a terrible disaster would turn out to be one of the most fortunate things that ever happened to me.

Chapter Two

The world you come from tells you a lot about where you're headed.

I was born in 1928 in the Bronx, and in September of 1929 the stock market crashed. You think that was a coincidence? I didn't even own any stock, being as I was only a year-and-a-half-old. Fortunately, my parents didn't own any stocks either since my father worked as a streetcar conductor and my mother stayed at home with my older brother and me. In fact, they were so poor, they couldn't even afford to give us middle names.

When my parents came to the United States, they were so pleased to be in a country which guaranteed freedoms, especially religious freedom, that they wanted to assimilate. So they gave all their children English names and that's how I got the name Arthur. Most of the Jews coming into the U.S. in those days had the same feelings about what a great country it was to be in and they wanted other people to believe they were going to fit in.

My father came to the United States from Lithuania in 1900 when he was five-years-old. When he was a small boy living in the ghetto in Lithuania, like all Jews had to do, he was kidnapped by gypsies. As he was literally being led away never to be seen again, one of his neighbors recognized him, chased the gypsies off, and took him back. I came *that* close to never existing.

My mother came from a little village that today is inside the Polish/Russian border called Tourgawelke bei Strei which is on the Strei River. She wasn't exactly sure how old she was when she came to America and could only remember that she was a young teenager. My parents met in New York City. It was never clear how they got together, but I'm pretty sure it was an arranged marriage. It was important to Jewish immigrants at the time for everyone to stay within the Jewish community.

When I was born, we lived at 898 Fairmont Place, which was right near Tremont Avenue and Southern Boulevard. As an adult I found out from my cousin that his wealthy father owned the building and that my parents didn't pay any rent, which is good because I'm sure they couldn't afford it. Today the building is gone.

I never met my father's father, who died of cancer before I was born. I know he owned a haberdashery in New York, though my grandfather had been a grain merchant back in Lithuania and for some reason he had farming in his blood. Eventually, he saved enough money from his business in the city to buy a 300-acre farm in the Millington Green Township of East Haddam in Connecticut. Sadly, my grandfather died before he and my grandmother were able to move there.

Jews are traditionally known as doctors, lawyers, jewelers, some kind of businessman and the interesting thing is that most Jews stayed in the city … but my father became a farmer! How many Jews came to the U.S., the land of opportunity, to become farmers? Do you know of any? There were some Jewish families in Moodus and East Haddam, and Sprecker Dairy, the dairy in town that processed their own milk was run by Jews. It was the first pasteurized milk I had. I count about eight Jewish farmers in our area. I'm sure there were more in the state of Connecticut. I remember a chicken hatchery in Guilford run by Jews. That's where we bought our chicks to raise for laying hens and broilers.

A few years after my grandmother and father arrived on the farm in 1913, World War I broke out. My uncles Barney and Herman, who helped run the place, lied about their ages and joined the military — leaving my grandmother and father alone to run the farm. After thirteen years, my father and grandmother and my mother moved back into New York. My mother didn't like the isolation and primitive farm life.

We eventually moved back out to Connecticut in 1931 when I was three because my father could not stand the city any longer. Our apartment on Fairmont Place was right across the street from a street car barn, but what my father loved was being outdoors, working outside, and he just liked being on a farm — so off we went, back to Moodus, which means "place of noises" in the local Indian dialect. At that time, the whole township had about 2500 people, and the new farm my parents bought had about eighty acres.

That old farmhouse wasn't much, built in 1800 in the old barn construction method. It didn't have insulated walls or framed construction, just planks against beams, and when that was done, they put the lath on the inside and plastered it. It had the old 16-by-16 windows, made with original 1800 wavy vintage glass. We had no running water except for a hand pump in the kitchen, no electricity, no central heat, just two wood-burning stoves. We didn't have a car, just a horse and buggy to go to town. We had an outhouse, no inside toilet. One thing I remember quite clearly is that the winters were colder than hell! Nothing in that house was insulated, no weather stripping, no storm windows. It was drafty and cold! Our main source of heat was one of the stoves, an old parlor stove in the living room that we loaded up at night with logs. In the morning we'd run out there and put our arms around the stove to get warm.

Despite all of this, I never remember once going hungry or not having warm clothes to wear. In the fall with some help, my dad would cut firewood for the two stoves, sometimes as much as forty cords. When I got big enough, I would help with the wood. I remember using a two-man crosscut saw with my dad. Shortly after we moved there we got telephone, electricity, and inside plumbing. Talk about moving up in the world! Even when we did get running water, we used to see ice in the toilet — it would freeze, inside the house! The barn outside was even colder than the house; one time I remember it was thirty below. We didn't get central heat until after World War II. Many times our plumbing froze up in the winter.

We grew all kinds of vegetables for ourselves, and eventually we got sixteen head of cattle for milking cows. We also had chickens. We sold broilers, eggs, and milk to a milk company. We sold maybe eighty gallons of milk a day.

I had a lot of jobs on the farm, most of which I wasn't too fond of. It was my job to clean out all the manure from the barn and to throw hay down from the rafters of the barn to feed the cows. I also had to throw silage down from the silo. The silo had rungs that I climbed up and little doors that fit in and closed it up. As the silage went down, I'd take out a door, pull out another one, and that's how the silage went down in the winter time.

One of my least favorite duties was weeding. I hated weeding frigging carrots. Carrots are very fine when they come up and I had to pull out all the weeds. I helped plant the potatoes and then we had to hoe the damn things to get out all the weeds. When it was time, we harvested them with a three-pronged potato hook. The trick was to dig on the side of the mound and try to get the potatoes out of the ground without piercing them and destroying them.

My dad did all the work around the farm with a workhorse. I remember him plowing the fields by hand, walking behind the plow and workhorse. And he cultivated with it. We took the hay in on a wagon and he'd pick it up by hand with a pitchfork, which I still can't believe — we're talking about a man who was only 5'4" tall! When he worked my grandmother's first farm out on Millington Green as a teenager, he would cut railroad ties by hand — each tie weighed like 300 pounds — and he would put them up on a wagon and then walk twelve miles to the railroad station with two pair of oxen in the wintertime. The reason he walked was simple: that wagon moved so slow, he'd freeze to death if he sat still and rode on it. He was an incredibly strong guy. But he was also a tough disciplinarian and was not overly affectionate.

Chapter Three

As a kid, I never went through that period of time where I didn't like girls like some young boys do. Luckily, my fifth-grade teacher, Miss Sullivan, thought the best way to discipline me was to make me sit with the girls. Talk about the fox in the henhouse! Unfortunately, anti-Semitism was pretty prevalent at the time and two girls in school thought it was cute to go tell Miss Sullivan that I beat them up at recess. She sent me to the principal, Royal O. Fisher, who was a sadistic prick. His daughter was in my class and *she* used to call me a "Jew son-of-a-bitch."

Anyway, one time I was sent to see the principal for supposedly terrorizing these girls and he strapped me. When I got home, my dad also strapped me because I was sent to the principal's office. He didn't want to know why, didn't want any excuses, he didn't ask me anything. That was hard for me. I also remember around the same time, my mom and I would walk to town. Part of our route took us under a big maple tree near where a Polish family lived. Well, the kids who lived there thought it would be funny to hide up in this tree and dumb pails of water on us. When I told my dad about it, he got pretty steamed. Though he was only five-foot, four-inches and these guys were six-footers, he went to their place and told them to leave us alone. He made it pretty clear that he wasn't going to take any crap from them, and these kids believed it. He wasn't a guy who would get in fights and he would stand up for us, but still one-on-one he couldn't show any affection. That's just who he was.

He was always into baseball, and he took me to the fourth game of the 1937 World Series between the Yankees and the Giants at the Polo

Grounds. The Giants won that game, but the Yankees went on to win the series that year. I know that he cared about me; he just didn't know how to express it. He also had a habit that if he was upset with us, not only would he punish us, but he wouldn't talk to us for a whole week. That hurt more than anything else.

My brother, Marvin, is three years older than I and my sister, Edie, is twelve years younger. Marvin was crippled on the right side of his body. I was never sure if he was born that way or if it was from a bout of polio shortly after he was born, but it severely impacted his life. His right arm was shorter with a weakened hand and as a young boy, he had to have surgery on his right leg, which left him with a permanent limp. At the age of thirteen, he developed epilepsy. I, on the other hand, was physically fit and life was much easier on me. Unfortunately, Marvin's physical disability affected his mental outlook and over time he became very jealous of me and bitter in general. He used to fight with me all the time. My dad used to tell me, "Don't fight with him; just run away." So whenever he'd get angry and want to beat me up, I would just run off and hide in the hayloft or somewhere else.

Things were not easy for Marvin. Because he was Jewish, had epilepsy, and was disabled, kids in high school would torment him terribly. Once, they tripped him and broke his two front teeth. If he would have had access to some kind of firearm, he would have gone and shot up that school, he was that angry. I never remember him really being happy, even later in life raising his own kids. His son once said to me, "I can't believe you two are from the same family." He blamed my father and mother for not sending him to college. They would have sent him, but they needed him to fill out the application and apply and he never did that. He was very bright and excelled in math, but rather than using his ability to achieve something that would help him make something of his life, he didn't do anything, and blamed his problems on everyone else. He became so difficult to deal with that my parents finally gave up and quit asking him for any help on the farm.

He was difficult to love, and I was a naturally-affectionate person, so my mother paid more attention to me. She would constantly hug me and call me "zin in tomas," which I think means "my sun in the sky." Don't ask me what language it is, but it always reminds me of the comic W.C. Fields who once said, "When I was a young child, I was so bright my mother called me Sunny."

My sister was born in 1939, and she immediately became my father's favorite. Her real name is Ethel, named after my mother's grandmother, Bubba Etela. But she calls herself Edie. I remember going to Middletown, Connecticut to pick her up at the Middlesex hospital when she was born. We drove there in a brand new 1940 Ford pick-up that we'd bought for $650. I was back in the truck bed and my mom and dad were in the front and we picked Edie up and brought her home. To this day, she won't talk to my brother because when he babysat her, he used to go out of his way to terrorize her and scare the hell out of her whenever he could. That was the way he acted with her, and she still hasn't forgiven him.

My brother, my sister, and I called our mother "Mama." I can still remember her cooking and baking on the wood stove in our kitchen. She used to bake challah bread, eggbread, and would always make a special small loaf especially for me as a treat. One day she forgot and when I asked her about it, she took a full-sized loaf and gave it to me. She was tough when she had to be and had a great personality. My father always brought her along to negotiate loans when he'd buy things for the farm because she was such a shrewd businesswoman.

She was a very hard worker, just like my dad. On the farm she milked cows early in the morning in all kinds of weather and did all the cooking. She was also a woman who got sprayed by a skunk and killed it with a broom outside the kitchen window one day. Once she got a snake wrapped around her arm when she reached down to pick up a pile of laundry she'd just taken from the clothes line. She grabbed it by the tail and whipped it into the nearby fields. She was very funny and could cuss and curse people like you wouldn't believe. My father would get very upset with her when she would let loose in public. She let people have it in Yiddish and a combination of other languages, often making up her own words. I don't think anyone knew what she was saying.

She had expressions for everyone and some were insulting as hell. Now typically Jews are not allowed to put curses on people, so these expressions are supposed to be kinder than a real curse. She spoke some Polish, some Russian, some German, and of course, Yiddish, which is 75 percent German, but she mixed up the languages. When I'd repeat her expressions to other Jews, they would look at me funny and say, "What does that mean?" When she would say goodbye to someone she would say, "Geh gesunde heit hachen ein guten schlet weg." And people would say, "what does that mean?" They knew that "gesundheit" meant "go in good health," and "haben ein guten schlet wegs" meant "have a good pathway." Even when I go on auditions I say those things to people.

Her brother Harry was kind of a crazy guy; he was a real philanderer. I saw his son about twenty years ago when his daughter got married who told me that once when he was back in New York, his father had a prostitute in the back of car and made him sit on the bumper until he was done. Harry was something else.

Harry's wife was from Hungary and wasn't very smart, so my mother nicknamed her "ein ungartisher pferd" which means "a Hungarian horse." It sounds funnier in Yiddish for some reason. As a man gets older, his testicles hang lower and when my father would wear shorts, she said, "Die alte cocker hat schittere yeiches." An "alte cocker" means an "old shitter" and the whole expression means "the old shitter has loose balls." ("Yeiches" is Polish for "eggs.") She'd also say, "wilde hyea von die Monashtane." I don't know where that comes from, and I'm not exactly sure of the meaning, but a "wilde hyea" is a wild animal from either somewhere out in space or another planet.

She used to have interesting insults for people. If she saw some woman she didn't like she'd say, "Sie kicht aus vie a crimmer perga" and my dad would freak out because it means "she looks like she has a crooked pussy." And when something happened that we were complaining about, that we should have done this or should have done that, she said, "far fallen vie nechtatin tag" which means "it's over like yesterday, forget about it." "Ferblungit" means "fermischt" or "all screwed up."

There were a lot of others she used to say, curses, stuff like that. "Er zol vaksen vi a tsibeleh, mit dem kop in dred," which means "you should grow like an onion with your head in the ground" or "Ich glach die wie a geshuin oft mein hinten," which means "I like you as much as a boil on my ass." One time a salesman was trying to sell her extra #10 cans. Now #10 cans are really big cans; you can't open them just to feed a family, because they are so large the food will spoil before it can all be used. During the summer, we'd use #10 cans all the time at the resort. Well, this one salesman was trying to sell all his stuff at the end of August with the season ending on Labor Day. She got really angry and after he left said, "That dirty sonofabitch, they should hang him in the electric chair!" Now that's double jeopardy!

I had to speak Yiddish to Grandma, my father's mother. She lived with us until I was eleven or twelve, and then she moved in with my uncle Herman. I haven't spoken Yiddish in a long time now, but years ago when my wife and I didn't want our kids to know what we were talking about at the table we used to speak Yiddish. Shirley also had a grandmother whom she spoke to in Yiddish.

My first childhood memory is of feeding some chickens that hung out by an old shed not far from our kitchen. I was barely three but wanted to be helpful, so I decided to feed the chickens some whole kernel corn. I filled an entire pail, but I guess it was too heavy because I dropped it and spilled all the corn out in the dirt. I panicked because I knew I would get punished, so I ran and hid in a nearby shed, crawling over all over the junk stored in there and squeezing into a very tight place in the back. Several hours passed and I started to hear voices. I looked through some spaces between the wallboards and saw all sorts of people scurrying around. I quickly figured out they were looking for me, so I crawled out. Someone picked me up on his shoulders to show everyone that I was safe and sound. That evening, I remember sitting on my father's lap. He was never an overly emotional man, but I'm pretty sure he was happy that I was okay.

Chapter Four

When I was a kid, I used to go out and pick wildflowers for my mother. Of our eighty acres, thirty or more were just pastureland — hay and open fields. There was a little brook that ran way up at the other end of our woods and fed a small pond where I used to collect pollywogs in a jar. During the summer in Connecticut, fireflies come out in the evening and we used to collect those, too. I'd walk alone in the woods a great deal. I would climb my favorite hemlock tree where I would sit and watch and hear the birds sing, and listen to the babbling brook as it went by. To me, that was entertainment.

One of my chores was to go out in the woods and find our milk cows and herd them back into the barn at the end of the day. We had a German shepherd named Major who I took with me to help herd the cows. Major loved his work a lot more than I did. He would chase the cows so fiercely that they would run into trees and jump fences just to get away from him. One time he had hold of a cow's tail and went right over the fence, never letting go. The only downside was that when the cows ran too much or got excited, it caused them to lose their milk. For this reason, after a while my dad told me not to take Major with me to get the cows anymore. But Major's reputation was well-established by then. If I was walking in the woods and couldn't see the cows, I would just yell Major's name and the cows would run straight into the barn.

One thing I really hated to do on the farm still haunts me. It was my job to kill chickens for food. I'd chop their heads off with an ax on a stump;

the head would still be on the stump and the body would run around in circles bleeding out until it died. To this day that still bothers me.

Even though I had a lot to do and had some great times, I was very lonely on that farm. Edie wasn't born until I was twelve and Marvin and I never got along. If I wanted to see a friend from school, it was a mile-and-a-half walk into town. That was far enough in the summer, but in the wintertime it was really not fun because it got so cold.

Despite my loneliness, I found plenty of ways to amuse myself. I liked to go swimming at the Neptune Twine Mills pond down at the Moodus River. The mill, built in 1850, was run by the Talbot family, whose son Kenny was one of my classmates. The mill was run with water wheels and in the pond was a pole that we tied between two trees about fifteen feet in the air. We used to climb up to the pole and jump off into the water. The only downside was that the pond was full of leeches. Every time we got out of that pond, we had to check our legs because the blood-suckers would attach themselves to the small of our ankles.

In the winter we would ice skate on the pond. Once I went out on the ice near the edge of the Moodus River with my cousin Saul Klar. I was wearing big hip boots and suddenly the ice cracked and one of my legs went right through and the boot filled with water. When I got home, my father strapped the hell out of me for going out on the ice. Everybody I knew went out skating, but he didn't care; he was worried I was going to drown.

Several incidents in my childhood were close calls where I could have been injured or killed. When I was ten-years-old, I fell out of an old tree and hit a stone wall. I sustained a fractured left wrist. I think I broke some stones, too. I went sledding with my cousin Dave down a steep hill that ended in a gravel bank dug out below. He said, "You go first and I'll watch from here." I climbed up and sledded down. I flew off this cliff, sailed off the sled in mid-air, hit the ground on my stomach, and slid down the rest of the way. I must have fallen fifty or more feet. I almost got killed and Dave was laughing hysterically in the snow on the ground. Lucky for me there was a lot of snow where I landed that prevented me from getting injured.

No one could afford skis, so we would take barrel staves, the slats of wood from the sides of a barrel, and then take a piece of leather and nail it to the stave. Our plan wasn't too successful because the ski would only have five or six inches of contact with the snow, so we had no control at all. Most of the time we'd start off fine, but after a few seconds we'd end up tumbling and rolling down the hill. Somehow we still managed to have fun.

Sometimes near the end of the summer we'd dig up potatoes from the fields, and then go out into the woods and build a fire. We'd wait until we had hot coals, and then we'd bury the potatoes and bake them. We also used to pick wild strawberries. They would come out in June or July, and they weren't a helluva lot bigger than big blueberries, but they were very tasty and very sweet. There were other people who had secret huckleberry bushes, but no one would ever tell us where the heck they were and we never did find them.

Some kids and I built ourselves a tree house in the woods. It wasn't really much of a house, more like a platform in the trees, but we'd go up there and hang out and have a ball. Another fun pastime was climbing to the highest beams in the barn where we kept the hay and would have pillow fights. We'd knock each other off and sometimes we'd fall twelve or fifteen feet until we hit the hay. We used to climb Mt. Tom, half of which belonged to my cousin's family, the Klars. Dave Klar was my first cousin, and we used to swing out over the cliffs on grapevines on the side of Mt. Tom like Tarzan. Unbeknownst to us, every time someone would swing, the vine would loosen a little bit from the top of the tree — until eventually my friend Stan Kouric swung out and the vine came completely undone. Stan fell and rolled all the way to the bottom of the mountain. He survived, but was scratched and bruised quite a bit, so we quit the Tarzan stunts after that.

In addition to working on the farm and having fun when I could, I went to school fulltime. They didn't have a kindergarten in my district, so I officially started in first grade. They would not allow any Jewish teachers in the school system back then. Finally, the Board of Education let the wife of Sam Pare, who owned a clothing store in town, become the fourth-grade teacher. She was the only Jewish teacher in the whole school.

In school, I was the class clown. I was in constant trouble with the teachers for speaking when I wasn't supposed to. My seventh-grade teacher, Miss Mathews, was always on my case because I was such a jokester. Once Mr. Belanik, who was the coach and also taught a history class, got mad and said, "If anyone talks or makes one sound, I'm gonna come over and smack you." In those days, corporal punishment was permitted.

Well, at the same time I accidentally dropped something on the floor and said something to somebody and he came over and whacked me right in the face. I'll never forget that.

I taught myself to drive in a 1929 Model A Ford pick-up truck when I was twelve years old. Talk about an antique — it had nineteen-inch wire wheels with very narrow tires. It was one of the first models to have a self-starter, which was located on the left-hand side down on the floorboards. Just to give you an idea of how simple this car was, Henry Ford requested that the packing crates he received his parts in be made in a certain way so that he didn't have to manufacture floorboards for his cars. He could just reuse the wood from the crates! It was a four cylinder, 30 horsepower engine, water-cooled, and still had a crank in front in case the starter didn't work. The gasoline tank was right up in front by the windshield, with a glass gauge inside so you could always see your gas level. The reason that the gas tank was that high was because there was no fuel pump; gravity moved the gasoline from the tank to the engine. If you were low on gas going up a hill and stalled, you would have to turn around and back up the hill so the gasoline would level out in the tank. The windshield swung open full so you get fresh air inside in the summertime.

Starting an old car like that could be quite an undertaking: you would use a key to turn on the ignition, turn a choke knob all the way open to create a rich gasoline mixture, then pull the choke out, and step on the starter simultaneously. Sometimes it started and sometimes it didn't. Sometimes you might crank it until the battery died and the batteries weren't that great in those days. If this attempt to start the car failed, it was time to use the crank! That entailed opening the choke, precisely adjusting two levers under the steering wheel (the spark level and the throttle), then going outside and crank. You had to be careful with that crank, because sometimes after you'd crank it, it would kick back and could break your wrist or your arm. After you got the car started, you'd jump back into the cab and adjust the spark and throttle and the choke and you were finally ready to drive. It had a three-speed transmission on the floor. I'd studiously watch my dad drive and do my best to remember what he'd done afterwards. I'd usually head out into the fields to practice. It had mechanical brakes and you could never seem to adjust the rods on all sides so that the brakes would pull evenly; stopping was a major chore! The brakes didn't react the way modern hydraulic brakes do; they were very slow. You had to plan way ahead where you were going to stop if you wanted to stop without crashing into anything. You probably would have stopped faster if you threw an anchor out or dragged your feet along the ground. If you got it going fifty miles per hour or more, you were really screaming. Everything rattled and made noise. There were no shock absorbers as we know them today, so it was a bumpy, noisy ride.

When I got good enough, my dad would let me go out on the highway. There weren't many cars on the road those days, and even less after World War II started. I used to run errands for my parents and take my mother to Middletown to go shopping. My father hated driving her into town, but I loved to drive because I was only twelve! I finally got my first driver's license in January of 1944 when I was sixteen. I doubt that many people today remember learning to drive on a Model A Ford.

Television hadn't been invented. In fact, the first television I ever saw was at the RCA Building in New York in 1945 when we went into town on a high school class trip. On the radio we'd listen to *The Shadow, Fibber McGee and Molly, Jack Benny,* and *Fred Allen,* among others. We didn't have any books in the house because my father and mother couldn't afford them; they had their hands full in the Depression just feeding us, but I never remember going hungry. I used to sit on my dad's lap and he would read me the Sunday funnies from the *New York Daily News.* We got the *Middletown Press* also. That was entertainment; you'd listen to the radio or make your own fun. That was it.

My uncle Herman, my father's younger brother, also lived with us until I was about eight. Herman didn't work; he was on disability pay because one of his hands got crushed by the dump on a big coal truck that he drove in New York after he returned from World War I. I used to sit on Herman's lap while he told me war stories. He served with General Pershing in the cavalry chasing Pancho Villa in Mexico before the U.S. entered the war. He told me one time he fell off his horse into a cactus in Mexico and they had to pick stickers out of his butt for a week. When the U.S. entered World War I, Herman went to fight in France. While he was living with us, Herman decided he wanted to buy a colonial house on about twenty-six acres near us in Moodus, but he needed three thousand dollars so he asked my grandma. After getting my father's permission, she loaned him the money and he bought the house. Then he married a woman named Frieda and my grandma moved in with him. Grandma died in 1939, at the age of eighty-eight. The day she died, she had been out milking the cows that morning. I guess you could say they grow 'em tough in my family.

Interestingly enough, after World War II started Rubey Bernstein asked Herman to run his liquor store while he served in the army. Herman loved that; he loved to schmooze with customers and he liked the booze, too. As it turns out, Rubey never got his liquor store back because when he came back from the war, he suffered from post traumatic stress disorder — at least that's what we call it now — and he never recovered. Herman continued to run the store and eventually sold it and retired with my Aunt Frieda. Over the years he became increasingly senile, or as my mother would say, "leuva buttle." He would collapse on the front lawn and Frieda would call an ambulance because she said he'd had a seizure. My father said he was more likely drunk, which was probably the case because he was a heavy drinker or "shicker." Then Shirley Elkins, his niece, came onto the scene. With Herman's mental condition deteriorating, Shirley grasped the opportunity and got Herman to leave everything in his will to her. After Herman died, Frieda was left to fight Shirley Elkins for her right to keep living in her part of the house. I suggested she get an attorney, but she said at her age it wasn't worth it, she didn't want to fight with her family and that the attorney would get most of the money anyway.

Frieda was always a heavy smoker and when she hit about eighty, she got a bad cold and the doctor suggested, "You know, Frieda, maybe you should quit smoking." She did. Meanwhile, Shirley Elkins was patiently waiting in New York for Frieda to die so she could sell the property and collect all the money. On one of my calls to Frieda to see how she was doing, she was very joyful. She told me that Shirley Elkins and her two sisters who were waiting for her to die were all gone. She'd outlived all the bastards!

My other uncle, Barney, who had also left the farm to fight in World War I, wound up in the Balloon Corps. In World War I, they used balloons for observing the enemy. They were tied down by cables and were easy targets, so it was a very dangerous duty. Barney survived, and when he came back to the U.S. he was kind of a ladies' man, or so I was told. My mother said more than once that I took after him. He landed a job as bell captain of the brand new Pennsylvania Hotel in New York. It was a very prestigious job, and Barney made big bucks; I guess he wore silk shirts and dressed very nicely. The guy was always running around with women and never got married. One summer day, he was on his way to the beach with three gals in the car. They got in an accident and the car's wooden steering wheel pierced his chest and killed him.

Chapter Five

*History repeats itself. Maybe because no one
was listening the first time around.*

Since I'm guessing most of you weren't alive at the time, let me just say the 1920s were a pretty wild time in America. The decade was dominated by two Republican presidents, Warren Harding and Calvin Coolidge. Harding's administration was known for its corruption, the Teapot Dome oil scandal probably the most famous. Harding didn't play by the rules on the home front, either. In the White House, his wife and a staff member caught him having sex with a White House aide in a closet! Coolidge was known as "Silent Cal." His famous quote is, "What you don't say won't get you in trouble." The Roaring Twenties, as they became known, sped up the conditions for the collapse of the economy leading to the Great Depression. The eighteenth amendment, or Prohibition, made the production, sale, and distribution of alcohol illegal in the United States. Despite its intentions, Prohibition increased the consumption of alcohol and helped lead to a big increase in organized crime. The speakeasy, the flappers, the Charleston and the Jazz Age flourished, and morality took a big hit. The telephone and radio were just coming into their own.

By the time the 1930s came around, the Depression was in full bloom. President Hoover tried to pass legislation to turn things around, but it was too little, too late. He did start the construction of Hoover Dam and various public works projects, which were expanded a great deal by President Franklin Delano Roosevelt. FDR didn't take office until January of 1933 when the Great Depression was at its worst. Prohibition ended in 1933 with the passing of the twenty-first amendment, which ended thirteen years of a huge mistake. The use of alcohol was legal again, but it didn't excite me that much because I was only five-years-old when Prohibition was repealed, although I would have a sip or two of wine at Passover. I remember having a beer when I was thirteen and my friend Irv Axelrod's parents owned the Log Cabin Bar and Grill in town, and he would bring booze to some of our high school events.

FDR enacted many laws to try to get the country back on track economically. New rules to govern the banks, the stock markets, the CCC, the WPA all kept people off the streets and put them to work doing something constructive. My father went to work for the WPA for twelve dollars a forty-hour week. Surplus food was given away at the high school. During this period of my boyhood, prices for food were very low: eighteen cents for a dozen eggs, jumbo sliced bread was five cents, four pounds of bananas were nineteen cents. Spring lamb was seventeen cents a pound. Gasoline was ten or twelve cents a gallon and there were no such things as self-serve; a guy would come out at the service station and crank the pump by hand. Social Security was passed and was objected to by the conservatives (even back then!) as being socialistic and an institution that would drive insurance companies out of business. In fact, it had the opposite effect because for the first time it made people aware of needing a retirement fund. Social Security became the basic fund, but it didn't provide enough to retire on, so people bought more retirement policies. I think Social Security is here to stay.

Until I was about twelve, I had a bed-wetting problem. All the laundry had to be dried on the clothesline outside and my sheets were outside every day. One of my uncles, who shall remain nameless to protect the innocent, would visit us and tease me constantly about my problem. I will never forget how embarrassed he made me feel for years. I didn't know whether he was a little off-center but one thing he did was talked about for years.

My uncle had a farm not far from ours. I guess he decided to burn down the house and farm and collect the insurance. This was in 1933 during one of the lowest points of the Depression. It was all his idea, but he talked his wife into doing the deed while he was in New York City. He took my dad with him to provide an alibi. The plan was doomed from the start. His wife left almost every clue you could imagine to indicate the fire was deliberately set. She used kerosene to start the fire, buried the silverware outside to save it, let all the cows out of the barn at night. Let's just say it didn't take the authorities very long to put two and two together. When my uncle returned from New York, his wife was in jail, there was no place for him and his family to live, and to top it all off, he never collected any insurance money and his sister held the mortgage. My father had to put up our farm to guarantee my aunt's bail. What a mess. The case never went to trial because of legal technicalities in place in those days that protected a wife from having to testify against her husband. After everything blew over, he rented a rundown house for a while and then they eventually moved in with his parents on their farm. Talk about a case of extreme stupidity!

A massive hurricane hit Connecticut in 1938 and took out everything including our barn, all the sheds, our silo; it even blew down three-hundred-year-old trees that were around our house. The house survived but that was about it. In 1941, we lost the two-story chicken coop. Back in those days we used kerosene heaters called brooders to keep the chicks warm. One day my brother was supposed to be watching the brooders and keeping them properly adjusted. He got distracted and the brooders overflowed; the whole two-story coop caught fire and burned to the ground. Just like that we were out of the chicken business, and the hurricane had put us out of the cow business — that was pretty much the end of our family farm. My father did build a small cow barn from lumber salvaged from the silo, large enough for about eight cows, but as the 1940s rolled around, our farm became a summer resort.

Chapter Six

*Don't let hard times get you down; opportunity
comes in different disguises.*

During World War II, people couldn't really travel anywhere overseas.
At first we'd just have our relatives come up and visit us. They'd pay us a
little something for the time they stayed there. From that, we built cabins,
a new dining room kitchen, a place to entertain. Our resort was called
Hilltop View. We had a spring that supplied our water, but in dry years it
was pretty touch and go, so finally we had to drill an artesian well, which
supplied about thirty gallons per minute. We also built a swimming pool
for the guests to enjoy. It started slowly, but pretty soon became a full-
blown resort.

My mother was a great cook; she had dozens of recipes that Jews
brought with them from eastern Europe, things like borscht and flanken,
and of course, brisket. She used to make apple cake and streudel and all
kinds of delicious things. When we became a resort, my mom was the
main cook. Eventually she hired her sister Annie to help her out. Annie was
the favorite of the whole family and was also my mother's favorite sister.
Together they did all the cooking and baking, and I can still remember
their story-telling and the way they always laughed together. Annie was
also an excellent cook, maybe even better than my mother.

Many times after working all day, my mother would come to the rec
room and sing for the guests. There were times we had chefs come in from
New York and we used to hire chambermaids and other support staff
from the city because people in town didn't want to do that kind of work.
Sometimes, we used to get prisoners on good behavior from Cheshire State

Prison in Connecticut to help out. Other times I had to go into Hartford to these bars and find guys to work but they were all alcoholics ... oh, I hated doing that! But I'd go pick them up if they wanted a job; they'd wash dishes, clean rooms, other low skill jobs. Some of them were such heavy drinkers that they would drink the vanilla extract in the kitchen just to get a little alcohol in their systems, get drunk, and off I'd go back to Hartford to go pick up another one.

I really didn't care much for the guests who came to stay with us, particularly the ones from New York. They'd come up and bargain with us to death on the price of the room and everything else. Then I'd see them sitting in the dining room, watching them feed their kids. It was always a fight with the parent saying, "I'm paying for this stuff; you're going to eat it!" and the kids not wanting to and then having it stuffed down their throats. Even then I said to myself that when I had kids I would never treat them like that. One thing I did like about the guests was the cute girls who came up from New York with their parents. Every couple of weeks I had a new girlfriend.

I started high school in September 1941, in the same building as the junior high except a new school, called the Ray School, was added. Some benefactor with the last name of Ray left money in his will to build a much-needed addition to our school. It had shops: wood, metal, automobile, drafting, printing, and agriculture and science labs. It was the first time anyone in high school had lockers, although we still didn't have a gym. I took every shop course available. I loved working with my hands and got a great deal of satisfaction from seeing the finished product. I turned a baseball bat out of ash. I still had it until the fire almost seventy years later — a handmade baseball bat that I'd made in 1941 was still in great shape. Later in life, when I needed a job to finish my bachelor's degree I got a job on a turret lathe because of my experience in high school on an engine lathe. I really think I would have been some sort of mechanic if I hadn't gone into teaching. I was not a great student; I only got good grades in the subjects I liked, the shop classes and the science classes. I did poorly in English, history, and math. I think my overall GPA in high school was C+. During this time, the war raged on in Europe. Even though the U.S. didn't initially get involved, we supplied Britain with ships and armaments and then of course, Japan bombed Pearl Harbor on December 7, 1941, which brought us into the war.

There were only three sports at my high school: soccer, basketball, and baseball, all boys only. All the smaller high schools in Connecticut played soccer because it was cheaper than football and they didn't have to pay for all the expensive equipment and pads. Also we could only field teams for sports with smaller rosters because our numbers were so limited. The only team I qualified for was soccer where I played fullback. The playing field was built by the WPA and was gravel. No grass, no sprinklers, no nothing. They didn't even rake all the stones off, so it was pretty rough. Our uniforms were flimsy shorts and shirts, no pads, no cups, and the shin guards didn't stay on so nobody used them. Our shoes were leather and the cleats fell off so easily and wore down so quickly on the gravel that we'd put a nail right through the middle of them to hold them on better. Lots of times before the game was over, you'd feel the nails coming through the bottom of the shoe. If someone from the other team dragged his shoe down your leg after a kick, the nails left scratch marks all the way down. Games were never called because of weather. I remember playing in snowstorms when you couldn't see more than twenty feet ahead of you down the field. You could hear other players out there running around and kicking, but forget about seeing where the ball was coming from. Suddenly it would come flying at you out of nowhere. If you got kicked when it was really cold out, you would feel some pain, but when you got inside and your blood warmed up, it would really hurt!

A lot of kids experiment with smoking — we used to make pipes out of acorns. We'd find big acorns, dig them out, put a straw into them and then we'd find old cigarette butts and dig out the tobacco and try to smoke them in our pipes. It would work okay at first, but they didn't hold up too long because the fire from the tobacco would burn right through. We also tried smoking corn silk, which was terrible! It didn't make us high or anything, we just smoked it because it was available. I was told later that marijuana grew wild out in the woods where we lived, but we didn't know about it so we never had the opportunity to smoke any.

Recently I reconnected with Carrie Turner, an old high school classmate who remembered some of the high school plays I was in and said I was pretty good. I don't even remember! According to her, I had the class hysterically laughing all the time. We were in high school during World War II and she said sometimes I would place a little black comb under my nose and come out the stage saying, "Sieg Heil" and a bunch of gibberish that sounded like German, imitating Adolf Hitler. Our teacher, Miss Haney, would start to bawl me out for wasting rehearsal time, but then she couldn't control herself and would start laughing also. She was our drama coach and also our English teacher. In those days females wore pretty short skirts, and she'd sit up on her desk and cross her legs and all the guys would position themselves so they could look at her legs, not listening to a word she was saying. During high school the only transportation available to me was my dad's 1940 Ford pickup, the one we'd picked up Edie in from the hospital. It was the only vehicle we had on the farm and the day of the prom, my dad and I had been hauling cow manure all day. The manure piles had been stacking up all winter and when you break into it in the spring, it's pretty ripe! Since it was the only vehicle I had to pick up my date for the dance, I spent the longest time cleaning that truck to get the manure smell out. If it did smell, my date was very polite and never mentioned it. The springs in the front seat were sticking through the upholstery, so we had to cover the seat with old blankets to make it halfway comfortable. Luckily we didn't have to drive very far, not only because of the lack of comfort, but because gasoline was rationed during World War II. After the prom, we went to some friends' house. We wound up in the upstairs bedroom necking, or "making out" in today's language. I thought I was going to really get lucky until the father of the house came home and threw us all out!

In high school, I loved the summers because even though I had to work at the resort, I got to go swimming. Once I got my driver's license I had to drive the guests at the resort to Bashan Lake, which was a real beautiful lake not too far from the resort. At first I drove a station wagon, but that got to be too small so we bought a 1946 one-ton truck and we'd put the guests in the back where they could sit down.

I remember once ice skating on a little pond near the high school where the kids used to gather. We'd build a fire to keep a warm. One night as I skated away, I didn't realize that the whole bottom of my pants had caught on fire. At the time there was a popular song that went, "I don't want to set the world on fire ..." Well, the next week the school paper quoted that line and then went on to say, "Why start with your pants, Art Frankel?"

World War II began when I was in high school and men started being drafted into the army. The country really rallied together after Pearl Harbor. On the home front there were all sorts of drives — metal, paper, blood; we were encouraged to save almost everything and recycle. There wasn't any plastic to speak of, but I remember toothpaste tubes were important to the war effort because they were made from zinc. Many things were rationed: meat, butter, cooking oil, sugar. Let me put it another way — there was very little that wasn't rationed. All production went to the war effort. There were no new cars or appliances; a piano factory near us was converted to making gliders for the air invasion. You couldn't buy new tires; you had to recap your old ones. I don't think anyone went hungry or suffered that much; in fact, on the home front people made more money than ever before and anyone who wanted to work could find a job. "Rosie the Riveter" was an expression that came into being when women took over mens' jobs working in the factories. People saved a lot of money because there was nothing to spend it on; you couldn't go overseas and travel was limited in the United States. That's one of the reasons my parents' summer resort did so well during the war years. Three of my cousins fought in World War II: Morris Frankel was in the Marine Corps and his brother, Teddy, was an officer in the army. Teddy won the Distinguished Service Cross for his heroism at the Battle of Guadalcanal. He lost a lung in that fight, but he survived and lived into his 70s. My cousin Marty Braun piloted the small landing crafts in the D-Day invasion of Normandy. He told me he spent two full days with no sleep ferrying troops from the larger ships to the beaches with artillery shells exploding all around him. His landing craft was finally hit with a shell; he was blown overboard but was not injured. D-Day, June 6, 1944, was his twenty-first birthday. Nice present.

Chapter Seven

By the time I graduated high school in June of 1945, the war was winding down. I was planning to join the paratroopers because I thought it sounded exciting. What I didn't know about was the 50 percent casualty rate. Ultimately, my plans didn't really matter much because by the time I got out of school the war in Europe was over. The war in the Pacific was still being waged, but I was only seventeen so my parents said they wanted me to stay and work on the resort for the summer. Our deal was that once the summer was over, if I wanted to I could still enlist. I reluctantly agreed to one more summer working at the resort and then in August of 1945 we dropped the bombs on Hiroshima and Nagasaki and the war with Japan ended. I thought, "Well shit, they don't need me now, the hell with them!" So my brother and I hopped on the train from New York to Miami; we were going to Florida for the winter and get jobs.

The dentist in Moodus, Dr. Friedman, knew someone in Miami Beach who had an attic that we could rent, and that's what we did. I worked as busboy, delivered groceries, even in front of a hotel operating a jackhammer. I also landed some work at a gladiola farm where the mosquitoes were like dive bombers. My brother never did get a job; the only place he worked was putting in a few hours at the gladiola farm, but other than that, he didn't do anything. I had seven jobs in seven weeks to survive. One week we didn't have enough money except for juice, coffee, and toast in the morning so we ate coconuts for a whole friggin' week! We even got picked up by the police because we happened to look like some guys who'd robbed a dry cleaners. When we were down at the police station they found out we were from Connecticut, which just made it worse. "Well, well; a couple of damn Connecticut Yankees!" At that time, and still to this day in some places in the South, people are still fighting the Civil War. Luckily, someone came in and determined that we weren't the guys they were looking for.

We stayed in Miami until November in that cramped, dark attic with no air conditioning. We came back home and my draft card was still 1-A and I really didn't know what my next move would be. I never intended to go to college because I thought only idiots went to college. You have to remember that back then we didn't have any counseling; the principal didn't give a shit about any of the students, the vice-principal was a full-time teacher and none of them were good at counseling anyway. Lacking any other clear-cut plan, I enlisted in the army. The war had officially ended, but hostilities had not yet been declared over so — at least in the army anyway — they allowed us to enlist for just eighteen months. And that's exactly what I did.

Chapter Eight

Don't get caught up in the little stuff — and
like the guy said, it's all little stuff.

I reported to Fort Devens in Massachusetts and was put in the Army Air Corps. This was the closest thing we had to an air wing of the military as the air force wasn't created until the end of the 1940s and the Air Force Academy wasn't built until the 1950s. I was sent to Keesler Field in Biloxi, Mississippi for basic training. To put it bluntly, Keesler was a hellhole. The food was terrible. The two-story barracks were halfway decent, but all the new recruits were assigned into one-story fifteen-man barracks. There were shutters but no windows, no air conditioning, and these crummy gas heaters. When it got cold the gas heaters came on, but then it would get too hot and everyone would be sweating, so the heaters would be shut off and then we'd get cold again. Walter Winchell's son got pneumonia down there and died. Winchell would always end his program with, "if your son's overseas, write to him; if he's at Keesler Field, pray for him." Finally I got moved to the two-story barracks.

At Keesler I ran into a guy from my hometown named Jack Axelrod, who was a little older than I was. Jack turned out to be the biggest con artist; he could talk people into stuff, and get things done. One Friday night after KP we went into Mobile with some other guys to raise hell and have a few beers. We went out, had our fun, and the next morning I woke up sick as a dog. Somewhere along the line I'd gotten ptomaine poisoning, and I was hurting. I told the guys, "I'm going back to the base." On the way to the train station to head back to Biloxi, I was feeling so bad I keeled right over on someone's lawn. The guy whose house it was came out, tried to talk to me, but I literally couldn't answer, so he decided I was just another drunk serviceman. He called the airfield in Mobile and got them to come out and pick me up. I was so sick, I had to have two days of intravenous feeding in the hospital. I recovered and returned to base.

I was now in the same phase of training as Jack, so I transferred into his squadron. We immediately got into trouble. He talked our captain into letting us go home for Passover. Jack told him, "All these guys get to go home for Christmas, we're Jewish and we'd like to go home for Passover." At the time we were right in the middle of bivouac, which is when you go and live in a pup tent out in the woods and learn to live in the field off of C-rations. You could sleep one tent with two guys, or make it into four sections with two other guys. It is humid and rainy as hell in the winter down there in Mississippi; you're supposed to dig a trench around your tent so if it rains, the water will run away from your tent. One end of our tent was up against a tree and there were roots so we couldn't dig that deep. Since Jack and I got permission to leave, we happily took our tents away and left. We found out later that the other guys got flooded out right after we left.

On the way out, our captain said to us, "I'm giving you guys a special privilege. If you're one minute late coming back, I'm gonna court-martial you." Well, we shrugged him off, went down to the tarmac, caught a plane to Washington, D.C., and then another one to Mitchell Field in Long Island, and caught a couple of trains out to Connecticut. We stayed a few days, had fun, and some good meals.

One problem is that when you're in the service you're used to talking to other guys, and when you get home you forget how to speak civilly and you say stuff like, "Would you pass the fuc — would you pass the salt, please?" I had to watch myself around my mom, that's for sure. While we were there, the high school class had a field trip to Washington, D.C. Jack and I decided to join them, so we went to their hotel, partied with them all night, drinking and raising hell. Well, we didn't have a place to spend the night, so we went back to the airfield and slept on an old C-54, a hospital transport plane that was bringing soldiers back from Europe. It had five canvas bunks up high where they strapped people in. Without any other options, we went to sleep on this thing. Before long, we heard some noise; guys were coming on all causing sorts of commotion and we found out the plane was about to leave for Europe. Luckily we woke up or we would have had some serious explaining to do to our captain.

We got off the plane in the nick of time, and then started trying to find a plane heading back to Biloxi. We waited and waited ... to make a long story short, we got back late, a couple of days AWOL. We were scared because the captain had been pretty clear about our fate if we came back late. We kicked it around and decided there was only one hope. We went down to personnel, transferred out of our old squadron and into a new one. We were behind on a phase of training because we'd been gone for five days — so we transferred out and never saw that captain again! Somehow things have a way of just working out for me.

After high school before I went in the army, I dated a girl named Elaine Greenberg. I liked her very much and I think the feeling was mutual. When I wrote home to my family, nobody ever wrote me back, but Elaine always answered me, which I greatly appreciated. When I came home on leave my parents were very upset because they heard about all my activities and adventures in the army secondhand from her — they didn't stop to think that maybe if they had taken the time and answered me I would have written back to them! But they never did. Just a couple of weeks ago, I ran into Elaine Levine, her married name, on a website called "high school classmates." Before that, I hadn't seen her or contacted her for close to sixty years.

Most of my time in the service was a big joke. After Jack got a medical discharge, I got sent from Keesler Field to Geiger Field in Washington state and then on to Brooks Field near San Antonio. We went up to Geiger on an old troop train that had an old-fashioned coal steam engine, and for some reason the windows were open. By the time we got there, all our hair and clothes were filled with coal dust that had blown back from the engine. Between delays and being sidetracked, it took us over a week to get up there. Servicemen in transit were the last priority behind freight trains because the war was over.

One thing I learned about the service is that when you got moved around, they never sent your records with you. After I arrived at Brooks Field, I went down and started talking to the guys and asked where the various planes were going. They told me that one of them was going to St. Louis for the World Series and another was going to Mitchell Field in Long Island. I only had a pass for fifty miles, which means I couldn't go farther than a fifty-mile radius from San Antonio. Well, knowing that nobody ever checked, I got on the plane headed for Long Island. After we landed, the captain asked all the guys on board if we were on furlough. I quickly wandered away because I didn't want him to see my fifty-mile pass.

I got home to Moodus, spent a couple of days, then caught a plane at Mitchell Field — but shortly after takeoff I found out it wasn't going to San Antonio, but was headed to Barksdale, Louisiana. Oh shit, I thought, I was gonna be AWOL again! In Barksdale there was a plane going to El Paso. Being from Connecticut, I wasn't exactly sure how far El Paso was from San Antonio, but I figured it couldn't be that far. Well, it was 500 miles west in the middle of the desert! After a night in El Paso, I got on a B-26 attack bomber that cruised about 300 miles an hour. The captain was flying alone, so I sat up next to him in the cockpit in the co-pilot's seat. As soon as we left the field, he dove down and started flying fifty to one hundred feet off the desert floor. There were tumbleweeds going every direction, jackrabbits running around — I thought it was a blast! I had no idea how dangerous it was. Once we were back in San Antonio, I went down to personnel and checked in, scared shitless, only to find out my records hadn't come in yet. They didn't even know I was gone!

After Brooks, I was sent to Langley Field in Virginia. It was a permanent base, brick buildings, and I was in a twelve-man room, but like Keesler, no air conditioning. A sergeant worked there at the PX serving beer, but he drank a lot more than he served. One time, he came back on a very hot night, and everybody had their beds rolled down, so all that was exposed were the white sheets. Well, he came in drunk as usual, leaned up against my bunk and started pissing right in the middle of my bunk! I screamed and yelled and somebody turned on the light and everyone was just hysterical laughing at me. He pissed my whole bed! He thought he was in the bathroom; he didn't know where the hell he was. I don't remember if he apologized the next day or not.

I flew in many different aircraft, from the B-25, which was the Billy Mitchell bomber that bombed Tokyo; one of them flew into the 82ⁿᵈ floor of the Empire State Building in 1945. I flew in B-25s, A-26s, C-47s, C-54s, C-82s, the AT6. The first jet I saw was when my squadron changed from P-51 Mustangs to P-80s. The "P" stood for photo reconnaissance. They could fly about 500 mph. The first jet I ever flew in was in 1967 on my way to Europe on a tour with a group of high school students. Once I was flying into Langley and I knew more about parachutes than anyone else on the plane. We were flying along and I looked out this little plastic window and saw that the starboard engine was smoking like hell. Sonofabitch, the plane was on fire!

The captain called back and said, "Private Frankel, make sure all those men have their parachutes on and they're adjusted properly, because we may have to jump."

I said, "What? Jump where?"

He replied, "Outta the plane." I looked outside; we were over the Allegheny mountains or the Shenandoah mountains and if we jumped, we were gonna land in trees for sure. I was eighteen years old, and had the shit scared outta me — thank God He feathered the prop, shut the engine down, and since we didn't have a lot of weight, he flew us into Langley on one engine.

After we got back, I was sent on temporary duty from Langley down to Lawson field in Columbus, Georgia where the 82nd Airborne trained. They were so crazy and wild — Columbus was right across from Phenix City, Alabama on the Chattahoochee River. Phenix City became a real den of iniquity. Interests from Chicago were down there running illegal gambling, illegal alcohol, you name it. They would find a body in the river almost every day. We went to Phenix City once. Someone had a car, and everyone was drinking. I was too drunk to get out of the car, but the other guys went inside a bar to have some more fun. Luckily I didn't leave the car, because fights broke out and it got as crazy as hell in there — guys humping girls on the dance floor; it was just really wild.

I had hay fever before I went into the service and I was getting immunization shots, so I asked the doctors at the infirmary — two Jewish interns who hated the army — about allergy shots. They told me they didn't give allergy shots there, but if I wanted to go to Oliver General Hospital in Augusta, the food was great and they had their own golf course. To sweeten the pot, it was home to the Masters Tournament which was coming up. I said, "Sign me up!" So they sent me to Oliver for two months — and they tested exactly two days out of the whole two months I was there! They had the ninth hole and the eighteenth hole on the golf course roped off for special men like me who were convalescing from World War II. I played golf on their course, hanging out in my convalescent garb. I would run down the slope, jump over the ropes and settle into a lawn chair and people would whisper, "Gee, I wonder what's wrong with him?"

Some of the guys in my ward were there for gonorrhea, some of them getting it for the second and third time. There was one really cute nurse in our ward; she'd walk by and this one southern guy would say, "God, that's eatin' stuff! Anyone who would stick a dirty old dick in that would be violating the Pure Food and Drug Act." Nobody ever said servicemen were known for their tact or civility.

While I was there I got to see the 1947 Masters and Byron Nelson, Gary Middlecoff, and Babe Zaharias. I was in Augusta during Passover and I was invited over for a Seder with a local Jewish family. I even had a date with a Jewish girl while I was there. When it was time for me to be discharged from the hospital in June of 1947, I only had two months to go in my hitch. They didn't think it was worth sending me back to my squadron, so I got out early with a full eighteen-month credit for my service. I had the World War II G.I. bill, and got three-and-a-half years of college out of it. But that was my service time in a nutshell, flying around the country getting into trouble. In total I got one day AWOL on my service record out of all those times I was absent without leave.

Chapter Nine

Find the right partner, and you'll be the richest person alive.

After getting my discharge, I went back to Connecticut without much of a plan and wound up working another summer at the resort. The guests aggravated the hell out of me worse than ever. The New Yorkers were very demanding, and some of the women were so spoiled. I really had enough of it all, but I didn't know what my next move was going to be. Once again, good fortune came my way. I got a letter from Irv Axelrod, my army buddy Jack's brother. A bunch of guys I knew — Irv, Jack, Al Wang, Lou Mager — had all started college at Drake University in Des Moines. Irv wrote, *"Why don't you come out and join us? It's a really nice school, we like it real well."*

I thought it over, and remembered all these kids I'd met in the service who were from Appalachia. To them, the service was heaven because they had showers, running water, toilets, and three meals a day. You'd see them flicking the lights off and on in the barracks and flushing the toilets because they'd never seen them before. We all had to take a G.I. driving test. Out of thirteen guys, I was the only one who passed. How friggin' dumb were those other guys? They would just look at comic books and listen to shit-kicker music (as we'd call it in those days). I thought, *I don't want to end up like those guys.* So I changed my mind and decided to go to college. One of the best decisions I ever made.

I sent for a Drake application, the only university I applied to. They didn't have SATs back in those days; all you had to be was in the upper 75 percent of your class. There were only fifteen kids who graduated in my class, so somehow I ended up in the upper three quarters. I applied

34

and got in! It really surprised the hell out of me. I applied for my G.I. bill and got that all straightened out, and then after my big decision to attend college, I faced my next dilemma — I didn't know what the hell I wanted to study. All the other guys were taking business administration, so I signed up for that, too.

I drove out to Des Moines, pledged AE Pi, the only Jewish fraternity on campus, and became a full-fledged college student. At AE Pi, I ended up being the steward and got free room and board for a while. I got a lot of great things out of going to school, but one event changed my life for the better like nothing else ever has.

I met my wife, Shirley, in the spring of 1948. It was at a fraternity party; she was only sixteen and I had just turned twenty. For some reason she hung out with the kids at the college, probably because high school girls are usually more mature than boys at the same age. Also, she was taking voice lessons at Drake, studying opera and classical music, even though she was still in high school. She was 5' 9" tall from the time I met her and I never got over 5' 8". She was just ready to leave and she put her hand on my cheek and very softly ran it across my face and said something like, "How you doing, big boy?" She wasn't like that at all; she was an innocent Iowa girl. I didn't know that. I thought, *Boy, I'm in like Flynn with her!* We started dating — but we never did have sex until the day we were married.

On our first date I visited her at her house. I brought her a present, a record called "Little White Lies" by Dick Haymes.

> *"The moon was all aglow and heaven was in your eyes*
> *The night that you told me those little white lies.*
> *The stars all seemed to know that you didn't mean all those sighs*
> *The night that you told me those little white lies.*
> *I try but there's no forgetting when evening appears,*
> *I sigh but there's no regretting in spite of my tears.*
> *The devil was in your heart but heaven was in your eyes*
> *The night you told me those little white lies."*

That became our song.

The whole time we dated I'd ask her, "How come your mother is so short and you're so tall?"

She'd just reply, "Oh, my father was tall."

I couldn't know for sure because her father died of a heart attack when she was about five-years-old, but I'd look at a picture on the mantle and say, "He doesn't look very tall to me." I bugged her until she finally told me the truth — she was adopted. Believe it or not, there was kind of a stigma attached to being adopted in those days and she didn't want to tell me right away. My only reaction was, "Thank God you're not gonna look like your mother!"

Her adopted father had a taxi and rental car business with his brother. Interestingly, his brother had married Shirley's mother's sister — two brothers and two sisters. His brother and his brother's wife weren't the most honest people; they swindled Shirley's mother out of the business and she was left alone to fend for herself. She worked at Yonker's department store as a seamstress, and during World War II she worked at Fort Des Moines sewing for the military. Shirley grew up alone; no other brothers and sisters. Like me, she was kind of a lonely child, always wanting to bring animals home, but her mother didn't allow it. She wanted to bring people home to visit all the time.

She sang in the choir at her synagogue, and went to a high school near her home, but then transferred to Roosevelt High in the western area of Des Moines because she had friends there that she liked to hang out with. She played piano and had a very beautiful soprano singing voice.

We got married on January 21, 1950 when she was eighteen and I was twenty-two. Her mother wouldn't come to the ceremony. It wasn't because she was marrying me; she just didn't want to lose her baby. The day we got married, I had seven dollars in my pocket. When the ceremony was over I offered to pay the rabbi and when he saw how little money I had, he said, "Keep it; you need it more than I do!" The next day, Shirley's mother was so upset about losing her little girl that she asked her to leave, so we rented an apartment near Drake until the semester ended. I still had to take my finals. As you might expect, I didn't do much studying. We'd just gotten married and I'm sure you can figure out how we were spending our time. And I got my best grades ever that semester without even studying!

When the semester ended, we drove back to Connecticut and my folks gave us a belated wedding reception. We stayed with them, and Shirley and I both worked that summer at the resort. Although I took a printing class, I was miserable. Growing up, my father had been very domineering; when I went away to college I started to feel like my own man. But as soon as I came back with Shirley, he pulled me back in again to his world, working at the resort, doing a lot of things I couldn't stand anymore. Shirley wasn't any happier than I was and told me I needed to go back and finish my bachelor's degree. My dad wanted me to stay and inherit "the place," but I knew that just wasn't in the cards. Shirley and I worked there that whole summer and never got paid. They supported us, and I got some tips here and there, but by then I knew for sure that inheriting the resort wasn't part of my future. So we went back to Des Moines to finish my degree. I got my G.I. bill for college reinstated, which paid for tuition and books, and now that I was married, $75 a month for living expenses. We rented a cheap apartment not far from Shirley's mother's house. My parents bought us a 1949 Ford Club coupe for our wedding present, but when we returned in 1952, they asked us to sell it. They needed the money to put in a swimming pool at the resort. So I bought a 1931 Ford Model A coupe with a rumble seat for $75.

Our son Jeff was born on January 9, the second semester of my senior year at Drake. Right around the same time, my G.I. bill ran out, so I needed a job, particularly with a baby to provide for! At this point I'd gotten all my requirements out of the way and all I needed were fifteen elective semester hours to graduate. I didn't want to stay in Des Moines and take finals, so I asked the hospital to send me a telegram saying, *"wife and son in hospital in Connecticut; come home immediately."* This wasn't a lie, because she was there having a baby! I was getting good grades by then, a B average at least, much better than I did in high school. Some of the professors just gave me the grade I had at the time; others sent their finals back to the high school in Connecticut and let me take them there.

I still didn't have a job, so we moved into an upstairs room in my parents' farmhouse. Soon, I got a job at Hamilton Standard Propeller. When I applied for the job they asked if I knew how to use a turret lathe. I never had, but I'd had experience on that engine lathe in high school, so I told them I did and they gave me the job. My hours were from midnight to 8 a.m., six days a week. I registered at the University of Connecticut and took my fifteen semester hours, driving ninety miles a day back and forth between Moodus and Hartford. I slept about four hours a night, and was dead tired all the time, but somehow I did it. I was cutting big castings on the turret lathe, taking $5/100^{th}$ of an inch off at a time. It took a half-hour for the automatic feed to feed the lathe from end to end, so I would take my notes, stick them in my shirt, and while the lathe was working, I would go sit on the toilet and study. Sometimes on that midnight shift I'd fall asleep. The lathe had a sheet metal guard and sometimes guys would come by and whack it with a hammer to wake me up and scare the hell out of me. I thought the thing had exploded. I got a "C" average that semester, but I got my degree from Drake even though I finished up at UConn.

Shirley stayed at my folks' place during this time to take care of the baby. She'd cook for me. Once I told her I liked pineapple upside down cake and she took that to heart and we had it every week! She didn't know how to cook when we got married. She watched my mother and got some instructions from her. My mother wasn't the kindest person in the world to learn cooking from; if she didn't like what you were doing, she'd just say something in Yiddish and take the whole thing out of your hand. But Shirley learned how to cook on her own mainly because she cared about her family and wanted to feed us properly. She became a very good cook.

After I got my degree, I went to work at the Electric Boat Company in Groton which later became a division of the General Dynamics Corporation, the company that built the first atomic submarine, the Nautilus. Admiral Rickover was the one who put the whole project together. I was driving my brand new used Model A back and forth. It was a bumpy ride, but it got me where I wanted to go. Surprisingly, it was better in the snow than the newer model cars. In the wintertime, I would place an extension cord with a 100-watt bulb under the hood all night so it would start in the morning. They didn't have multiple viscosity oil then, so the oil would get like molasses on cold nights, and there was no garage to keep the car in.

I worked in the weight section of the ship design department. I didn't have an engineering degree or any training in shipbuilding, (although using proper naval terminology, submarines are referred to as "boats" and not "ships"). When I first started work there, I was surprised to meet a large number of carpenters. I often wondered, *What are carpenters doing working here on a submarine that's made out of steel?* Being curious, I went down to where they were working and found a complete, full-sized mockup of the Nautilus made out of wood. This was standard procedure for new model submarines. The engineers and designers needed to get a perspective of spacing to see how the equipment and people would fit in relation to each other. It's a lot easier to change a piece of wood than metal before the permanent equipment is welded in.

In the weight section where I worked, every plan drawn had to be submitted, including the materials used: steel, brass, fiberglass, etc. The bulkhead numbers had exact locations. My job was to figure out how much material, its density or weight, its exact location, its distance from the forward perpendicular or bow of the boat, and the distance from the keel. When the plans were finished and all the calculations were done, they were summarized and the total weight and center of gravity was determined. The engineers could then figure how much lead to put into the keel of the boat before launching. The rest of the weight difference was made up by the ballast tank. I was told they couldn't have an error of plus or minus 10 percent, although they were usually not more than 3 or 4 percent off.

I worked on the atomic submarine for two years. I was there when President Harry S. Truman welded his initials in the keel. I was there when Mamie Eisenhower launched it; I was right underneath where she broke the champagne. There were three bottles of champagne broken on the Nautilus. The first time she swung, it didn't break, and since they think it's bad luck if the bottle doesn't break, the captain broke one about midship, and somebody else broke another one, so in the end three bottles were broken that day. I remember jumping up on the platform after the ceremony and ripping my pants clean up the back; the whole seam tore out. I had to go back to the office and staple the seam back together along the inside.

But I wasn't an engineer; I wasn't trained. After all, my bachelor's was in business administration. Shirley and I decided that I should go into teaching so I could work at the resort in the summer and still have a full-time job the rest of the year. Shirley talked me into getting my master's, so off we went back to Des Moines where I enrolled in the Drake School of Education and began working toward getting my master's in counseling and education and so I could earn my teaching credential. To earn money, I substituted for a while and then worked full time for a semester as an eighth grade social studies teacher at May Goodrell Junior High while completing my degree.

While working on my master's we lived in a basement apartment. We managed the small building in return for free rent. There were all kinds of creatures living with us including cockroaches and mice. One Sunday morning we were both sleeping in when there was a knock on the door. We opened it to find a man standing there with Jeff and Nancy, who were about four and two at the time. He was the manager at the supermarket about a block away and had found them in his store with a shopping cart full of candy and cookies. It was wintertime, and Jeff had dressed himself and his sister in warm clothing and decided to go shopping. You might say Shirley and I were a little embarrassed.

After getting my master's we went back to Connecticut (where else?!) and I got a job in Mystic right next to the Mystic Marine Museum. The interesting thing about working there was the kids in my history class were related to the people in the textbook. Roger Williams, Israel Putnam — all these kids were descendants of the people we were studying!

In the fall of that year, Shirley and I had a difficult patch. We'd had our second child Nancy by then. Looking back, I really blame myself for any problems we had. I was the kind of guy who would get angry very easily and yell. Shirley, on the other hand, was kind of timid and I guess I scared her. She and Nancy took the train back to Des Moines to stay with her mother, while little Jeff stayed with my parents in Moodus. I kept calling her, but she wouldn't come back home. She didn't want to come back, but didn't really know why — she was very confused. I had a brand new little '54 VW bug by then, and over Christmas vacation, my sister and I drove out and picked up Shirley and Nancy and drove everyone back home. When I ask Shirley today about why she left, she says that she doesn't know why.

Chapter Ten

The fire that burned our house to the ground in October of 2007 wasn't the first time we'd had a close call. After all, we knew we lived in a rural wooded area where this sort of thing was a risk. In 2003, there was a fire down in San Bernardino that started to come up the hill. I drove out to an overlook on the Rim Highway that comes up the mountain and thought, *Oh, look at the fire down there!* We came home and didn't think much about it, when suddenly that afternoon the sheriff's department notified us we had to evacuate! I thought, *Oh shit!* Luckily, we were prepared for this type of emergency. Our daughter Rochelle was living us, as well as four dogs and four cats. We gathered all our necessary belongings, took all the animals and went down the hill and stayed with our daughter in Chino. Our neighbor Mike Ayotte, who'd adopted one of our cats, came with us, too. We waited it out and finally the authorities let us come back. When we returned home, the electricity was off and all the stuff in our refrigerators had spoiled. What a mess and what a stink! We finally cleaned everything out, got rid of the smell, and resumed normal life again. The fire had come within about a mile and-a-half from us. From that point on, we'd always look to the north and northeast thinking if we'd ever have a problem from a fire it would come from that direction. The Santa Ana winds blow from that direction and have a history of bringing trouble with them. And in October of 2007, that's exactly what they did.

Chapter Eleven

If things aren't happening where you are, change the scenery.

While we were in Des Moines, I saw a notice saying that the school district out in Henderson, Nevada was hiring. I applied because I thought Nevada might be a nice place to go. I drove all the way out there from Connecticut on Easter vacation of 1957, had an interview, and got the job. So in June we loaded up our few possessions, our two kids, and moved out west. Jeff was five and Nancy was three and Nancy rode the whole way out in a little cubbyhole behind the back seat. We arrived at our rented house on Brown Street in Henderson, which was right across the street from a titanium plant. The main street was dirt and gravel and the wind was blowing. There was a big dust storm coming down the street and it was 110 degrees outside. Shirley just looked at me and said, "You've brought me to hell!"

Henderson was the first place that we'd ever lived west of Iowa and it was still pretty raw and primitive. I took a teaching job at Basic High School teaching U.S. History and driver's education. I never taught driver ed and wasn't really qualified, but that didn't seem to matter to anyone in Nevada, which we found out later was typical of the Nevada education system. Talk about the wild west. A principal at one school didn't even have a bachelor's degree. In those days, the school system was dominated by people who either had a background in athletics or in the Mormon Church. The superintendent was a bishop in the Mormon Church. If you were either of those, you definitely had a leg up. Near the end of the year Michael Callahan, a school counselor, decided to leave education to enter politics. He later became the governor of Nevada. (Years later I was on the highway near Carson City with a fellow teacher from California and

I mentioned that I knew the governor, and kidding with him, said that maybe I should call him and see if he was in. Of course, he thought I was full of crap so I called his bluff, stopped at a phone booth, and called the governor's mansion. Callahan was in, invited us up, and we visited with the governor and his family for the rest of the afternoon.)

I had my master's in education and counseling, so I applied for Callahan's position and quickly received my first lesson in Clark County School District politics. A Spanish teacher with no background or training in counseling applied and got the position based solely on his qualification as a beer-drinking buddy of the principal. So I applied for and got a job at J.D. Smith Junior High in North Las Vegas and we bought a house in Las Vegas on Iowa Avenue right at the edge of the desert. When it rained all kinds of creatures wandered down in front of the house, including snakes and scorpions. Jeff enjoyed it because he loved to walk into the desert and collect a variety of insects and animals. In December of 1958 my daughter Debbie was born in Boulder City, a town near Vegas built for the workers of Hoover Dam. Then in December of 1959 Rochelle was born, not even a full year later.

In addition to teaching, I worked as a guide at Hoover Dam, about twenty minutes from Henderson, to earn extra money. I used to take out about four or five tours a day during summer vacation and during Christmas break. People from all over the world came to see the dam; in fact, one day I met some Frankels visiting from Israel who came from the same part of Russia that my dad had. It was a fun job; the only thing was lots of times in the summer the temperature would get near 118 degrees. Even after all this time certain facts still stick in my mind, like the dam is 660 feet thick at the bottom and 45 feet at the top. It's 550 feet down the front side of the dam from the top to the bottom where the spillways come out.

Lots of tourists had heard the rumor that someone was buried in the cement in the dam, which wasn't true. What happened was that between 1931 and 1935, when the dam was being built, some guy would leave the job and wouldn't tell anybody, and other workers would pour the cement in big sections. They would put pairs of shoes against the forms — and when the forms were removed, there would be the outline of shoe soles and somebody would say, "Oh, that's Joe; he got dropped in the cement." They used to play tricks like that, but nobody's buried in the concrete.

I got another job with the newly-built Danny Kolad Youth Center, built with donations and named after a boy who drowned in a boating accident out on Lake Mead and whose father ran the Desert Inn. Lake Mead is much more treacherous than people think. Because the air is so clear, you can look all the way across to the bank on the other side — which is twenty miles away — and think, "That's not very far; I'll take my boat over there." Boaters get out there and the wind whips up and suddenly they're in trouble. Lots of times bodies don't come up to the surface because the lake is ice cold at the bottom from all the snow coming out of the Rocky Mountains. They don't bloat; they just decompose at the bottom of the lake.

To help out, Shirley worked as a coat-check girl at the Sands Hotel. Over time, we got in good with Fran and Carl Cohen who ran the casino there. Whenever we wanted tickets for a show in Vegas, we got 'em free. On our anniversary Fran got us in to see the Rat Pack perform. She even sent a cake to our table. I remember standing behind Dean Martin once while he was playing blackjack and he picked up the cards and said, "Should he hit me?" I said, "Don't ask me, I don't know shit about this game!" Dean was very friendly and so was Sammy Davis, Jr.

Sinatra, on the other hand, was very arrogant and wild and he didn't give a shit about anybody. He owned a percentage of the Sands and one night he came in and started riding around the casino in a golf cart, totally drunk. The people running the casino decided that somebody should get Carl, because they couldn't handle Sinatra on their own. Carl, a pretty big, husky guy, came in and tried to reason with Sinatra, until Sinatra called him a "Jew bastard," at which point Carl punched out Sinatra's front teeth. After that, Sinatra sold his share of the Sands and got points in the Fremont.

The beginning of the end for us in Vegas began innocently enough. I was at synagogue one day talking to Hank Greenspan, who was the editor-in-chief of the *Las Vegas Sun* newspaper. In casual conversation, I started talking to him about the school system and how screwed up it was, how political it was, how unqualified people were getting promoted because of being drinking buddies with the principal. I didn't think much of it, until the next day all my comments were on the front page of the paper! Dr. Gray, the superintendent of schools, called me into his office and ripped me up one side and down the other. I said, "I'm sorry, but it's true. I didn't know they were gonna print the whole thing!" He threw me out of his office.

By then I'd had more than enough so I quit and started selling Prudential Life Insurance full-time with Norm Luani. Once Norm invited me to go with him to a reception where not only did they have a variety of food and drinks, they also had prostitutes that you could hire. One guy at the party decided to get a blow-job right in front of the whole crowd. The next day I read his name in the paper — he was a local boy scout leader! What happens in Vegas …

Even though Norm was a nice guy, I didn't really like selling insurance. I went back to Dr. Gray and said, "Look, I know we had our differences, but I'd like to apply for a job and come back and teach next year. I know you don't like what I had to say, so if I don't have a chance at getting rehired, say so now so I don't bother with it." He told me everything was fine, so I applied for a job but I didn't hear shit back. I told Hank Greenspan who wrote another column about how Las Vegas was losing good teachers because of the horrible way the school system was being run. So, in 1961, I applied for a job in San Diego.

Chapter Twelve

I quickly found out that San Diego was in a recession and wasn't doing any hiring. They did tell me that a little further north the Newport Beach School district was opening up a new school, Lincoln Jr. High School, in Corona del Mar, and was looking for teachers. I was hired to teach social studies and the Frankel family was on the move again. Unfortunately, I'd used up my G.I. bill on our houses in Las Vegas, and when we came out west we discovered we couldn't afford to live in Newport Beach. Instead we found a house in Huntington Beach for $17,500 on Enfield Circle for just $600 down. I didn't have the money, but they let us move in without paying the down payment. Pretty soon they wanted the payment, so I joined a credit union and borrowed the money. I asked the owners if they would take three hundred on the six I owed them and they said yes, so I got the house for $17,200. Today that house is worth $600-700,000.

My family loved the area, especially after coming from the desert. We'd go to the beach all the time, and on Sundays we'd pick up smoked tuna from the stands and get fresh corn on the cob for dinner. We loved to camp at Lake Cachuma up near Santa Barbara, and Holy Jim Canyon in Orange County. That was the cheapest entertainment and we had a ton of fun camping, backpacking, going to the beach. We loved California.

Lincoln's principal, Joe Edgington, was the only principal that I can say was really great. He visited our classes, evaluated honestly, gave good suggestions on how to improve our classes and stood behind us 100 percent if parents would try to come after us. His only shortcoming was that he drank too much. Every Friday night he'd say, "Come on; we're having an educational seminar," and then we'd go out to a bar in Corona del Mar. There were some nights I really shouldn't have driven home. But Joe really was a great principal.

During my time at Lincoln, I became a much better teacher. I started using game simulations where kids actually act out lessons in class. Kids learn much better by doing rather than being lectured to. We had activities about the Depression and the farm belt. I used another one about the Constitution, and the Articles of Confederation. I'd divide all the kids up into different states and have them charge tariffs just like the states did in the time of the Articles of Confederation and they found out for themselves what did and didn't work and why. They came up with new rules and learned how the Constitution was written.

I used to play tricks on the kids from time to time. Whenever we'd have a test, I'd "inadvertently" leave an answer key out in the open by the pencil sharpener. The first two or three were correct and all the rest were wrong. I'd leave it there and then go back to my desk and see them whispering to each other and nudging and then they'd all go up to sharpen their pencils and copy the whole test down. The next day, we'd go through the test and their answers would be all wrong and I'd just smile, "Gotcha!"

Another trick I played on them was very educational, at least I thought so. I cut out a round piece of cardboard about thirty inches in diameter. I numbered the outside of the circle with numbers from one to forty. Under each number I placed a picture of a president from Washington to Kennedy. Under each picture I printed all the pertinent information about the president. Then I'd place another piece of cardboard on top, its diameter cut smaller so that the numbers would show. It was attached in the center so that the inside circle would turn. Inside the circle I cut a window so that students could turn to any number and find information that pertained to that president. President Kennedy was number thirty-five, and since I'd written forty numbers, there were five empty places. By now I was clean shaven with a butch haircut, but when I was in Nevada, I had a full head of hair with a moustache and a Van Dyke beard. I looked like one of those South American dictators. I had a picture of me from Nevada, put it in the blank space next to Kennedy, and in the window space I asked the question, "Who is the famous American patriot pictured above?" All year long they researched in the library but never guessed it was me. At the end of the school year, I told them and they took it very good-naturedly. How much do you think they learned trying to find out who that guy was?

On a very sad note, I was teaching at Lincoln School when the news came over the loudspeaker that President Kennedy had been assassinated. I couldn't control my emotions and had to step outside where I broke down.

I had a great group of kids. Buddy Ebsen's kids were in my class. I honed some of my acting skills by trying to keep them interested. Sometimes I'd throw in corny jokes like, "Why were Spanish ships so economical? Because they got 10,000 miles to the galleon."

This was also during the Vietnam War era. Like a lot of people, at first I bought the government's rationale as to why we were there, but after a while I decided it was a big mistake. The way the world looked to me back in the 60s, the communist countries would slowly turn toward capitalism and some or many capitalist countries would accept elements of socialism and we would not be that extremely different from each other. It looked like we headed that way without the war. When countries trade with each other there's very little chance for animosity. China and Vietnam are two communist countries that are excellent examples.

Lincoln was located in Corona del Mar, a very conservative area. One of the problems we had was the John Birch Society, a political organization known for supporting ultra-conservative causes. I was discussing different people who might be running for president with my class and a guy named General Edwin Walker, known for his conservative political views, was one of them.

Suddenly I got a message through the principal. "You shouldn't be talking about the presidency and the elections" — it was a social studies class!

I said, "If they want me to tell the students what the John Birch Society is all about, have them bring in the *American Opinion* magazine (the John Birch Society magazine) and I'll read sections so that the kids can get both sides of the story." One of the kids did. Some of the material in the magazine said that Eisenhower was a Communist, and that John Kennedy was killed because he wasn't turning the country over quickly enough to the communists. After reading several different articles, most of the kids just looked at me and shook their heads in disbelief. The John Birch Society was very active during the Vietnam War. They even had these summer camps for kids; they didn't call them Hitler Youth camps, but they were just about the same!

In 1961 my mom and dad finally decided to sell the resort because they just couldn't handle it anymore. They wanted me to take it over, but

I just couldn't. I didn't really want to do it. I know this was hard for them to accept. My dad had never wanted me to leave to begin with; to him it was so important — "the place, the place." Jews were kind of educated inadvertently in Europe that land was important. They were never allowed to own it during the Middle Ages, which is why there were forced to go into medicine, jewelry, business, banking, become artisans. That was ingrained in their heads, that land was the most important thing and it was very difficult for them to give it up. I finally talked them in to moving out here, and with the help of the shop teacher I built an apartment in the back of the house for them with their own bathroom, kitchen, and everything. We also added another room so our son Jeff could have his own space.

In 1964 our last child, Cindy, was born. To earn extra cash, I worked part-time selling *World Book* door-to-door in Corona del Mar and Harbor Island — very wealthy areas. One time I was in the Ahmanson home on Harbor Island; it had thirteen bathrooms. Sometimes my customers would offer me a drink. I'd get home half-snockered and Shirley would be holding dinner, quite angry, and who could blame her? My *World Book* manager gave me an old Chevy, a 1954 that wasn't running great, so a neighbor of mine and I took the engine out and fixed it. My father used that car to take Shirley to the hospital the day Cindy was born. I was teaching that day and joined them at the hospital later. Cindy was the smallest of all our kids, four-and-a-half pounds, and they wouldn't let us bring her home until she was five pounds; luckily, she's gained a little weight since then.

As evidenced by my experience in Las Vegas, most of the time, except for Joe Edgington, I was in trouble with all my administrators. For some reason it seemed that most, not all of them, but most, forgot why they'd gone into education in the first place. They got all involved with the money or the budgets or the parents bullied them and forgot they were there to help the teachers educate students.

When I was at Lincoln, I won a trip to Chicago for selling *World Book*. By this time Edgington had left and over the summer we'd gotten a new principal named Werner Carlson. I told him I'd won this trip and that to take it, I'd have to miss the first day of school.

He started in with, "Well, we're getting this new superintendent and we're going to have an orientation and blah, blah, blah." He basically told me I couldn't miss that first day.

Well school hadn't started yet so I said, "You know what? I'm going to take a sick day."

He looked at me and said, "If you do, you'd better come back with a doctor's note." He was so impressed with his principal's job, a former English teacher who struck it big.

I said the hell with him, flew to Chicago, met the astronauts as well as Sir Edmund Hilary — and while I was there, I got a note from a doctor in Chicago. When I got back the second day of school, I gave it to him. Since I had a note, there was nothing he could do about it, but he was pissed as hell! I guess it was just some of my leftover shenanigans from the service. I had other conflicts with administrators along the way.

At May Goodrill in Des Moines, there was a community fund or something like that … and every year the whole Polk County School District had 100 percent contributions, and I was told I <u>had</u> to contribute. I said, "You know, I'm barely making enough as it is, and besides no one tells me who I contribute money to. I'm sorry but that's the way it is." I said no to the vice-principal, and no to the principal; I went right up to the superintendent of Polk County. I never did contribute. I just hate people telling me who I have to contribute to.

Later, as a counselor at Fountain Valley High School, I was required to attend a special baccalaureate ceremony that was held for some of the kids before the June graduation ceremony. The main speaker was a local preacher who was supposed to give a non-secular inspirational speech. Well, this guy was obviously a devout evangelical and got all fired up about Christ. As he got himself worked up, he got more emotional and louder and louder, pointing at the students and yelling, "You will believe!" I was sitting right behind him on the stage and finally I'd had enough. I turned to the counselor sitting next to me and said loud enough for everyone to hear, "Who's this guy Christ he keeps talking about?"

Let's just say the administration didn't take too kindly to my remark. The vice-principal came up to me after the ceremony and said, "Art, next year we can have a rabbi."

I told him, "I don't want a rabbi! You don't get it, do you? This is supposed to be an inspirational event, non-religious. This is a high school, not a church. Have you ever heard about separation of church and state in our constitution?"

The principal also found me. Instead of apologizing and making changes the following year, he said, "Art, if you don't want to attend next year, I'll excuse you." These are the kinds of idiot administrators I put up with my entire career in education, from Connecticut to Nevada to California.

At one point during our time on Enfield Circle between our family, relatives, and friends we had eleven people living with us. This included my son's friend, Martin Harvey, who'd just come out of the service; his father and mother were divorced and he didn't want to live with either of them. My cousin Martin Braun was living with us; he was just coming off a divorce and that got pretty interesting. His soon-to-be ex-wife was mentally ill, no exaggeration. Before he left their house, he had a beautiful oak custom-made toolbox and she got angry and took an ax to it, just chopped it up. They had a VW bus with the sliding windows in the front. At one point she'd caused so much trouble that they put out a warrant for her arrest. When the police were trying to arrest her they chased her through the streets, and when she finally pulled into the station, the officer reached his hands into her car to get her keys, and she slammed the window on his arm. We weren't spared her insanity either.

To get even with me for taking in Marty, she called the police and told them that I was making obscene phone calls to her and I was a child molester who came on to her property without permission, all of which was, of course, false. At the time I was taking a German class, and one night I came home to find the police waiting in my house for me. They handcuffed me and took me to jail on her say-so. I was in the Huntington Beach jail until Shirley went to a bail bondsman and bailed me out. The police came the next day and listened to the tape she had made. Just to show you how nutty she was, they found out <u>she</u> was making obscene phone calls to <u>me</u> and cussing on the phone and I had never been over at their house at all. They let me out, but it still cost me for the bail bond. That's when I decided enough was enough. I'd found out that my next door neighbor's brother-in-law was building three triplexes at 16th and Palm in Huntington Beach, so Shirley and I talked it over and made an offer on them. We moved our family out, and we paid the rent on an apartment a block away for my father and mother. I knew I had to move, and it was the only way to get rid of everybody!

My parents lived in that apartment for a number of years, but slowly my mother showed signs of dementia, and became senile. I don't know why she wasn't diagnosed with Alzheimer's, but she had some sort of dementia. Eventually we put her in a home. She spent the last two years of her life there before she died in June of 1975 around the age of eighty. My father died four months later in October. My dad never did acknowledge that I had done a good thing getting my bachelors and masters until he came out to California. But he did finally tell me he was proud of me.

The triplexes had both advantages and disadvantages. We lived in one unit, and the rents we were able to charge from the other two covered our mortgage, but not much else. We also had to serve as maintenance crew, painting and making repairs, including fixing damages from a renter-caused fire and flood. The whole situation quickly became cumbersome and although by sticking it out we would have made a ton of money, I became interested in a sailboat and we decided to sell.

You may find the business side of this amusing; I certainly did. The first year we filed our taxes after acquiring the triplexes, we were audited … and continued to be for the next six years! I had a colleague at Lincoln School do my taxes and the audits were all settled reasonably. The seventh year when we sold the triplexes was incredibly complicated. Between equities, trades, and cash received it was an accountant's nightmare. My buddy knew he was in over his head and handed me off to an accountant he knew who was a former employee of the IRS. He was very aggressive. By then I'd sailed to Hawaii and back and he listed that as a deduction; he claimed my library was worth ten thousand dollars, and God knows what else! Naturally, I get audited and right in the middle of trying to get everything straight — my new accountant died! Can you believe the gall and chutzpah of the guy?! I'm kidding of course, but by the time the dust settled everyone, IRS included, admitted my finances were so convoluted and confusing that they were willing to settle the whole damn thing for $3000. They couldn't figure out what else to do! On a more somber note, I learned later that the wife and son of the accountant who passed away became homeless and had to live out of their car. Odd how his strange behavior benefited me, yet was a disaster to his own family.

Chapter Thirteen

*Life is truly an adventure; never allow yourself
to stop having new experiences.*

Something about me has always been attracted to adventures. When I was forty, a buddy of mine and I decided to hike to the top of Mount Whitney, which at 14,495 feet, is the highest point in the continental United States. It isn't rock climbing, but it is a very difficult, arduous hike with a lot of steep, rough trails. We decided to go in May — not a good time of the year to go as we found out, because when we got up to 13,000 feet the whole pass was completely snowed in. We must have had a good time because we went back up another time with my son and a friend of his from high school, who were fourteen or fifteen at the time.

The whole trick of walking up that mountain is to take your time because of the thin air as you gain elevation. Well, the kids didn't know any better; they went on, got way ahead of us ... and when they got up around 10,000 feet, they totally crapped out. One of them got altitude sickness. Carl, a fellow teacher, and I kept going, and the boys stayed down and waited for us. We made it to the top the next day, and from there we went all the way down to Whitney Portals at 8300 feet.

On the very top of Mount Whitney is a stone building, maybe ten by twenty feet. On top is a lightning rod which is attached to thick cables going down into the rocks. There's a big warning sign, "If you see clouds approaching, leave immediately because of the danger of lightning." Even though there are lightning rods, solid rock is not a good conductor of electricity. There are reports of people hiding inside the stone building during lightning storms and bolts of lightning bouncing off the inside of the walls. If clouds are approaching, the best thing to do is to leave or to lie down in a low place.

One thing that surprised us was that on top of the mountain, if you put bread crumbs in your hand, small birds would land in your hand and eat with no fear. I don't know what kind of birds they were, but there are chickadees, nuthatches, and snow plovers in the area. The Forest Service later told us they were probably rosy finches. When we were at base camp we had to protect our food any way we could, because there were lots of marmots. They're like little ground squirrels or chipmunks; they're terrible thieves and will just wait to steal anything they can.

You might think going up and down Whitney would be enough for most people, but as you've probably figured out by now I'm not most people. Just before I turned sixty-five, I went back one more time with my daughter Cindy, her husband Gordon, and once again, my son, Jeff. As if making it up that mountain one more time wasn't enough of a challenge, I carried a couple of six-packs of beer all the way up in my backpack. It was a lot of work and I was really dragging my butt, but we all had a beer together at the summit. For some reason going down was harder on me than going up. Every time I started to walk, my muscles burned like hell. I stopped and rested until the pain went away and then I started again — and the pain came back. All the way down it was like that. The others tried to wait, but I told them to go on ahead. After a while darkness fell and I used a flashlight to see the trail when Gordon came back to see where the hell I was. He ended up taking my pack the last couple of hundred yards. Somehow they'd figured out a way to make that mountain steeper over the years!

In the spring of 1971 my cousin Eric, who is about a year older than Jeff, came out to California for a visit. Jeff and I took him on a camping trip to Yosemite and then on to the Mammoth mountain area as we wanted him, along with Martin Harvey, to experience the spectacular scenery and wildlife of California. Our last stop before heading home was at a campground near Hot Creek, where many backpackers and skiers would stop by to relax in soothing pools before heading home. Hot Creek is part of a geothermal area that was formed around 750,000 years ago with the eruption of a giant volcano 2500 times larger than the eruption of Mount St. Helens. It collapsed in on itself and formed the twenty-mile long, ten-mile wide Long Valley Caldera. The water from the Sierra Nevada Mountains seeps down into the ground where it is heated by rising magma and then boils back up to the surface at Hot Creek.

Most of the people entering the creek were skinny-dipping. We joined in with the crowd and did the same. It was dusk and getting dark and nobody really cared. There were always a few wussies who wouldn't disrobe (like Shirley, the one time I took her there!) The night that we were there, it was jam-packed, like a big can of worms milling about. You could hear all kinds of comments and screams because the water could be very hot or very cold depending on where you were. Night fell and it became pitch black. It was kind of strange to talk to men and women knowing they were nude, but not being able to see the expressions on their faces.

I was talking to someone when all of a sudden some kid yelled, "Mr. Frankel, what are you doing here?" It was a student from the middle school where I was teaching at the time.

I just said, "The same thing you're doing — skinny dipping!" Then unexpectedly, a large bus drove up and a busload of people got out and proceeded to build a large bonfire near the hot springs. The evening was rather chilly so bathers started to leave the creek and warm themselves around the fire. The people from the bus were on a church trip and were fully clothed and apparently very naïve about the goings-on in Hot Creek. The group leader immediately got everyone back on the bus so that no one would be exposed to sinful behavior. Thank God they left their bonfire for us to enjoy!

I was 203 pounds when I was nineteen, the same when I got married at twenty-two. I got down to 195 over the years by not eating as much, but I didn't really start exercising until I was thirty-nine. I started running a couple of miles along the beach, then I got a bicycle, then I joined the gym. Now I have my own gym in the house and I work out at least three days a week. I'm very lucky, I don't have a cholesterol problem, and I have low blood pressure naturally. I feel very fortunate.

Chapter Fourteen

After Joe Edgington left Lincoln, it wasn't nearly as much fun to work there so I applied for a job at nearby Fountain Valley High as a counselor/ dean. The administration's concept of the position was that you were supposed to be a disciplinarian and a counselor. Well, I took them at their word that counselor/dean meant exactly that, so I would counsel first and then if I had to discipline somebody, I would. I had a colleague named Juanita Halloran and she was — well I think she always wanted to be a man or something, because that's how she acted. There were 4500 students at Fountain Valley and she was counselor/dean for half of them, while I handled the other half. She wanted me to go around and measure the length of the girls' skirts, and check if they were wearing bras.

I said, "You gotta be kidding me! I'm gonna check to see if a girl is wearing a bra?! Get accused of sexual harassment; get put in jail? I don't think so! If you wanna do it, go ahead." As you've probably guessed, we clashed right from the very beginning.

My theory was that if a kid had discipline problems he should be counseled and the teacher's side should not always be taken, because when something happens, it isn't always the kid's fault. One time, some kids came into my office with a note from the art teacher telling me to discipline them because they had told him "*f— you*." Reading the note, I couldn't help but smile.

I asked, "Did you really say that to him?"

They said, "Yeah."

I asked them, "What happened?"

Well, because of the huge student population, the school had double lunch periods, so while some kids had lunch, others were still in class. Near this art teacher's class were some kilns behind a chain link fence. These two boys would stand near the kilns and talk every day, and for some reason it bugged the hell out of this teacher — even though they weren't disturbing anybody.

One of the kids said, "We were standing there talking and he threw a pail of water at us!"

I said, "What? He threw a pail of water at you?!" The kid nodded and said, "So we told him 'f— you'."

I called the art teacher and said, "Did you really throw a pail of water at these guys?"

He said, "Yeah" and then he laughed.

I said, "In that case, you deserve a f— you!" Well, by the end of the year, the principal, Dr. Berger, and Juanita Halloran decided that I wasn't tough enough on the discipline, so I became just a regular counselor rather than counselor/dean.

Juanita was a real hard-ass. They didn't have air-conditioning in the schools in those days and sometimes when it was hot, some teachers would wear shorts. One Monday morning I came in wearing shorts and she came into my office and reprimanded me; she just went on and on. The next day, Tuesday, I wore long pants. Wednesday I came back in with shorts and she went ballistic.

She said to me, "You don't really care what I think about this, do you?"

I said, "No Juanita, I don't." That was it in a nutshell; she was into all this trivial stuff I just wasn't. She used to constantly put letters in my file reprimanding me even though teachers would always come to the principal and tell him about what a good counselor I was. Teachers, whose kids weren't even in my counselor load, would send them to me because they knew how good I was with personal problems.

On the last day of school there was a school picnic I didn't particularly want to go to, so I stayed in the office to keep an eye on things and answer the phone. I was sitting there with nothing to do, when suddenly I thought, *I know what I'm gonna do; I'm gonna go into my personnel file and see what's in there.* It was probably illegal, but I went to the secretary's desk, got the key and opened my file. Lo and behold, none of the commendation letters from the teachers were in there, but all the ones from Juanita Halloran about my insubordination were. I took all those letters out, threw them away, cleansed my file, put it back and no one ever knew. I guess I always had problems with authority or something; I don't know what it was.

I ran into some very interesting and poignant situations as a counselor. A girl who'd moved to the school from Arizona came to see me. Her mother had moved the kids for safety reasons because the girl's father was forcing the girl to have sex with him. The mother had been hospitalized in an accident when the girl was about twelve and her father started raping her because the mother wasn't available. She was telling me the story, and mentioned that her mother wouldn't let her get mail from her boyfriend back home. She wondered if he could send his letters to her to my mailbox so her mother wouldn't know. I said, "Yeah, sure." That was a mistake. It turns out her boyfriend was sending her marijuana and didn't want to send it to her house. And my mailbox was right outside the principal's office. I found this out and told her sarcastically, "That's really nice; are you trying to get me arrested?" That was the end of that, but a short while later I got a call on my voice mail from the FBI! I thought, *Holy shit — the FBI?!* I didn't want to call back, but I did. Boy, was I relieved to find out they were just looking for a recommendation for a kid who'd applied to a police academy; I thought I'd gotten nailed for sure!

Generally speaking, it was the same old story with that school: petty administrators, good teachers, bad teachers. A science teacher was sleeping with a student who had recently graduated. A couple of other teachers were having sex with the high school girls — one of my counselees was pregnant twice by the same shop teacher and nothing was ever done! A gymnastics teacher was having sex with another girl and I finally went to him and said, "What's the matter with you? You want to jeopardize your marriage, your career, not to mention go to jail? She's underage!"

I met the actress Michelle Pfeiffer when she was a freshman at Fountain Valley; she was about fourteen years old. She used to talk to me almost every day at lunch out on the quad. When she left high school, she worked for a while as a checker and then decided to pursue acting, and as they say, the rest is history! Years later when I was thinking about going into acting myself, I called and spoke to her father who told me, "She lives up in Hollywood now, but she comes down here all the time for dentist appointments. I'll tell her you called." Well, I never heard from her, so I called him back again and I've still never heard from her. Later when I was a working actor, I tried to contact her and congratulate her on what she'd accomplished because I think she's very talented. When she went to Russia to work on a film, I wrote her a letter and then a couple of years later I was on the Warner Brothers set when she was shooting *Batman*. I went to the production office, left a note with a card, but she never answered me. I came to find out later that she was kind of ashamed of her childhood. She came from Stanton, which is considered one of the low-rent districts in Orange County, and she just wanted to move on. If you ask me she had nothing to be embarrassed about; her father was a very reputable man — I believe he had an air conditioning and heating business — but for some reason she wants nothing to do with her days at Fountain Valley. I read once where she said she was a straight-A student, but I remember that she hung out with the surfer guys and was a C-student. I don't get the need for the deception. I'd be proud of coming from meager beginnings and becoming as famous as she is.

Somewhere along the road, I became friends with Bob Kane who created *Batman*, the entire comic book series. I was at his place once and he gave me an original lithograph of his original characters that he drew in 1939 when he started drawing Batman. He signed it, *"To my friend Art; bat's wishes, Bob Kane."* I don't have that lithograph anymore because my grandson, who is a real ardent comic book freak, mentioned how much he liked it, so I gave it to him as a present. He still has it.

Bob Kane told me that when they were casting the first *Batman* picture a well-known actress was being considered for the female role opposite Michael Keaton and Jack Nicholson. Well, it seems she'd had an affair with Michael Keaton, and she'd had an affair with Jack Nicholson. I guess the powers that be decided it would be kind of touchy having them all on the set together, so she didn't get the cast in the first *Batman* film. To me it's the first time I ever heard of an actress screwing herself ***out*** of a job.

Chapter Fifteen

Even if you think your dreams are impossible, try to make them come true anyway. You just might surprise yourself.

During my time at Fountain Valley High School I put into motion events that would lead to one of the greatest adventures of my life. In 1976 I bought the hull of a sailboat. But let me back up a bit.

I don't know whether it's an essential thing in people that we came out of the sea and we want to go back, but I guess I started feeling the urge when I built a kayak in high school. It was made out of wooden frames, copper nails, wooden stringers, and then covered with canvas and treated so it would be waterproof. It was heavier than hell, but it floated. I used to take it down to the Moodus River and paddle it around.

I didn't really venture out on the water again until I was in the service at Langley Field, which is right on Chesapeake Bay. There were little dinghies that the servicemen could check out. Other than my kayak, I'd never sailed before, but I took one out and figured out a thing or two and sailed around the bay. I guess I was starting to get hooked.

When I was at Lincoln, a fellow teacher had a twenty-six-foot volkboat. It had a Marconi rig, which is the typical configuration for most modern sailboats, with a headsail and a mainsail and was originally designed in the Netherlands. He also had a little eight-or nine-foot dinghy, which one day I asked him if I could take out. He said sure, so I took it out on Newport Bay and taught myself how to sail.

As you're probably starting to see, I've always done things by the seat of my pants; something will grab me and I'll say, *I can do that.* Shortly thereafter I bought my first boat, a nine-foot fiberglass Columbia dinghy with one sail. I'll never forget the first time I took Shirley out in it; it was windy and it was rough as hell. We launched it off the dock and were out barely ten minutes before I had to turn it around. We almost sunk the friggin' thing! But I wasn't the least bit disheartened and one day I was sailing around Newport Harbor when the city was having its annual boat show. There were these Westsail thirty-two-footers built for cruising — full keel, a double ender. Well, I got pretty jazzed up because those boats could cruise the world, they were that sturdy. That really got me going. I started doing some investigating and eventually decided I could do better. After a while, I found what seemed like the perfect opportunity. I found an ad in the paper from a guy selling a hull that he had started and had sitting in the water at Redondo Beach. It was modeled after a Kendall gaff-rigged ketch, which was designed by a man named William Atkin back in 1924. Atkin's son was still alive in Connecticut, so I got his number, called him up, and asked him how I should rig it. He told me everything I needed to know. So I bought the hull. And just like that I had a sailboat hull in backyard. Every spare minute I had went into working on that boat. I christened the hull the "Sarah Ann," which was the name originally given to Shirley on her phony adoption records. Phony adoption records?? Don't worry; I'll get to that story in a few short chapters.

The hull was fiberglass and came with the deck already attached. There was no gel coat on the outside, so I had it painted with an epoxy-resin paint. There was seven thousand pounds of lead in the internal ballast and it had a full keel. The Westsail thirty-two had the exact same hull. I was able to do a lot myself, but there were certain things that were just beyond my expertise. Jeff worked with me almost every weekend and holiday and I had a kid named Gary come up to do all the precision joiner work, the decking, and all the cap rails. That kind of work is tricky because on a boat, everything is a curve, nothing is square.

Gary had a problem of not showing up to work when he was supposed to. I remember several times buying him pot to entice him to come to work. Thanks to him, I spent every penny I had (and some I didn't) getting that boat built. He talked me into doing it all with wood. The deck was ¾" marine plywood covered with fiberglass, later covered with ¾" teak. The hull and deck were attached with a sheer clamp made out of five pieces of laminated mahogany. The cabin sides were made of 1 ½" marine plywood and then fiberglass over that, and then on top of that ¾" mahogany cabin sides. The cabin top was ¾" marine plywood, and then fiberglass and then ¾" teak. The cap rails were South American rosewood, the pin rail around the mast was ash, the top of the rudder was ash with trim pieces of ebony, the bowsprit (the pole extending forward from the vessel's bow) and all the spars were made of Alaskan Sitka spruce. The bowsprit had a platform of teak trimmed with a wood called perduke. Down below, the cabin sole was teak, the drip rails were teak, the overhead cabin deck beams were laminated mahogany, and everything else was trimmed with mahogany and teak. The dining room table was inlaid with hardwoods too numerous to mention. The outside trim was iron bark. It cost me a fortune — $65,000 — not counting $10,000 worth of equipment, which in 1976 was a lot of money. It still is!

The stanchions, all the cleats, the belaying pins, and the anchor windlass were solid bronze. They were all crafted in a bronze foundry operated by an eighty-year-old man in a foundry in Newport Beach. The cleats we used were bigger than some of the cleats I'd tie up to on the docks and people used to tease me about them. The ears holding the rigging I carved from wood, sand-cast them in aluminum, and then sand-cast the aluminum into bronze. The spars, two masts, the main and the mizzen, two booms, two gaffs, and the bowsprit were not everyday items you could find in a hardware store. I checked around the sailing community and finally found a wood lathe in Los Alamitos that was used for turning wood spars for the Navy in World War II. Not only did I find the lathe, but the same man who ran it back then was still there! The lathe was 105 feet long, and the operator sat in a chair with a cutting blade that ran the entire length and that's where I had my spars custom-made.

I also looked for parts at marine salvage yards such as Alaska Pipe and Salvage in Wilmington, California. While I was looking for parts for the boat, I ran across a bronze and silver bell from a World War II Liberty Ship. It weighed 125 pounds. I knew Fountain Valley was looking for a bell to be used as a trophy to be exchanged in their big rivalry football game against Edison High, so I bought it for six hundred dollars and was reimbursed by the school.

Now you're probably asking yourself how I managed to pay for all this on a school teacher's salary. Good question. Remember the triplex I bought when I sold my house to get rid of everybody? Well, I ended up buying three of them. I sold my house for $34,000 and then put 10 percent of $168,000 down on the triplexes. Even then I was still broke. The first year the property taxes came due on the triplexes, I didn't have the money for that, let alone building a boat. Once again Lady Luck smiled on me. A few years before, I had gotten into a land deal with some fellow teachers up in Shelter Cove, California, north of San Francisco. I had about $2500 invested. I went to the vice-principal at Fountain Valley and asked him if he wanted to buy my share straight across for the $2500 I'd invested. He just laughed like hell at me. But that's not the end of the story. Not more than a month later, the guy who got us into the deal traded the whole thing to the government for some other land, and I got a check for $13,000! I made a copy of that check and left it on the vice-principal's desk. I couldn't help myself; I had to stick it to him.

Now that I had some breathing room, I sold one of the triplexes to get started with the hull; then later I sold another one to keep going. I discovered the old joke about sailboats is true: "It's like standing in a cold shower ripping up dollar bills." (In case you're interested, the three triplexes I sold are now worth around two-and-a-half million dollars. Obviously, I wasn't concerned with the money.) I guess I have the philosophy of living life as it comes along and one thing I believe with all my heart: you're always going to regret the things you didn't do rather than the things you did do.

Eventually the job of finishing the boat got too big for the backyard. We moved it down to a boat yard in Newport Beach and we'd keep working on it after school and on weekends. The sails were heavy-duty marine Dacron. The boat came with a two-cylinder Volvo engine, I changed it to a three-cylinder Volvo diesel and it had eighty gallon diesel tanks and eighty gallon tanks of fresh water.

John Hanks was the technician who did the engine, insulation, and all the electrical. For the most part, John knew what he was doing — except when he was drunk. One day I remember him working in the engine room while I was up in the bow, and all of a sudden sparks and smoke exploded above-deck. It turned out he'd crossed the wrong wires — bet that really sobered him up!

We launched the "Sarah Ann" in April of 1976. That thing was built like a Sherman tank. It got so heavy that we had to raise the waterline. A Westsail boat was originally about ten tons displacement and when I put the boat in the water, the crane operator said, and "This boat has to weigh close to 26,000 pounds!" For the next two years we worked on completely finishing the inside and spent the rest of the time learning how to sail. My son came down and helped me all the time. I learned about celestial navigation and how to use a sextant because they didn't have GPS then. They had a system called Loran, but that was about $2000 and I didn't have the money. Using do-it-yourself Heath kits, I built the radio and the depth sounder myself and somehow got it finished. And that's when I decided to sail to Hawaii.

Chapter Sixteen

Our life in Lake Arrowhead prior to the morning of October 22, 2007 proceeded at a normal pace — me substitute teaching and acting, Shirley subbing. Until …

About five o'clock that morning, my neighbor Mike Ayotte called down and talked to Rochelle and said, "I can see what looks like the beginning of a fire way off to the distance to the north of me by Deer Lodge Park Valley." The Santa Ana winds were blowing really hard that day; I was told later they were gusting at seventy to eighty miles an hour. Shirley was scheduled to go to work at the high school that morning. I was up early and said, "Shirley, you'd better get up now, because the electricity is off; it's gonna take you longer to get ready in the dark."

We didn't have the TVs on and she came down, and suddenly the electricity came back on. We were puttering around doing our usual morning stuff around six or so when suddenly the phone rang; it was our daughter Nancy down in Chino. She was panicked and said, "They're evacuating up around where you are!"

I said, "What?!" We turned on the TV and she was right!

Almost immediately, someone from the sheriff's department called and said, "You guys are gonna have to evacuate." Mike called again and the next thing we knew officers came driving up the street, saying we had to evacuate. Although we couldn't see the flames yet, the wind was blowing horizontally and the smoke alarms in the house started going off — even though the windows were closed! The pressure of the wind was so strong against the windows that the smoke seeped in.

If you've never been in a situation like that, it's hard to understand the panic we experienced. We didn't know what to take, but Shirley had put all our photo albums out in the garage in a cardboard box. She also stuck my lederhosen in there and my Tyrolean hat that I had gotten in Europe; I figured those would be hard to replace. For some reason, she also put an old satin smoking jacket in there, I have no idea why; it was something I'd used thirty years before! I didn't know what to take. I did have a 30/30 carbine rifle and a twelve-gauge Ithaca shotgun, so I grabbed those because I knew ammunition in a fire was a bad idea. I had my original ship's log from Hawaii and I grabbed that out of a drawer, and grabbed all of my watches. You have to understand that they don't give you a timeline; they just say "LEAVE!"

I left behind twenty-two pairs of pants, and shirts. I did grab my two good pair of Lucchesi cowboy boots, but everything else, including a nice Fedora hat like the one my dad used to wear all the time, was history. You obviously can't take everything. We had a Russian samovar, a very fancy teapot worth $825 that was made in 1898 that Shirley's mother gave her. We lost that. We lost an old Mixmaster from the '40s that my folks used to use at the resort. We lost a lot of old letters, letters that my dad had written to my mom, letters I'd written to Shirley. As I ran out the bedroom door, my computer was there. I remembered that during the summer I had scanned 1700 family color slides onto my hard drive. I grabbed the computer, the keyboard, and the mouse and took them with me. Frankly, this fire was really starting to piss me off.

I had a glass room where I made stained-glass windows and right next to it I'd built a makeshift wine cellar with around one hundred bottles of wine. I thought, *Sonofabitch, I'm gonna grab some wine.* I grabbed five good bottles, came up into the kitchen and grabbed a big bottle of scotch and a bottle of gin and said, "Dammit, screw this fire; I'm having a drink tonight!" We took everything out to the car — but we couldn't find two of the cats. Shit!

At this point it was smoky and dark and really blowing and the fire was getting close. We finally found the cats and got them in the car. Rochelle was already a block down the street waiting for us, yelling, "Come on you @*%#&; it's coming!" As we backed out of the garage, the smoke was thick as hell. A Forest Service guy was screaming at us to, "GO!" Hot embers were falling on our heads and the garage door was open and for some reason, I wouldn't leave until I had the Forest Service guy close the garage. It didn't make any friggin' sense; the fire was right up the hill.

But he did it for me anyway. We drove away, went down to the end of the street, turned left, and went around a big U-turn and down to the next level where we could look up. We saw the flames coming down the hill toward the house and knew we were history. There went our dream house that we'd built at Lake Arrowhead.

Chapter Seventeen

To really get our sea legs and prepare for the journey to Hawaii, my son and I sailed the "Sarah Ann" around the Channel Islands, Catalina, Santa Cruz, and Santa Rosa. Sometimes the conditions got pretty rough, which was okay with me because I really wanted to be ready for whatever I might encounter out in the Pacific on the way to Hawaii. One day we were off Santa Cruz Island, where every afternoon in that area the wind whips down through the Santa Barbara Channel, and that day it had to be close to fifty friggin' knots. The bowsprit on the boat was twelve feet total and about eight feet off of the bow; we had netting that was made especially so that we wouldn't fall out. Jeff and I had the jenny sail up when all of a sudden a line squall came up and really started blowing like hell. Jeff went to take the jenny down and the boat was heeling so far the port cap rail was completely under the water. Meanwhile, he was up on the bowsprit and the water was up to his waist; we were really heeling with the decks awash. Even with me pulling up into the wind, it was blowing so hard he had a helluva time getting that sail down. I was holding the tiller as hard as I could, with my foot up against the corner of the cockpit just to brace myself — and finally he managed to get that damn sail down. My toe felt like it was dead, because I'd pressed so hard the blood had left my foot.

Around the same time I took up scuba diving because I wanted to be able to go down below if I had something fouled in the prop or other emergency. I was fifty then and by far the oldest one in the class — there was only other person besides me who took the beach dive test down in the surf at Laguna Beach and passed. As you can tell, I was pretty proud.

I did everything I could think of to prepare myself for the trip. We had an eighty-gallon fresh water tank and eighty gallons of diesel fuel tanks — I wanted to be sure we had a lot of extra fuel. I also bought a separate dinghy, a life raft, and a little outboard. I'd read things about ships being pirated by drug smugglers, so I brought along a 30/30 carbine Winchester that I'd bought in Vegas once after we were robbed, and I also bought an Ithaca seven-shot shotgun, a police riot gun, just to be sure. I got everything squared away, learned everything I could about sailing a boat — and in June of 1978 we sailed to Hawaii.

Chapter Eighteen

I looked around for someone to help me sail the "Sarah Ann." There was no way I could sail a gaff-rig by myself, and unfortunately, in the time it took to complete boat, Jeff had gotten married and had to stay home to help support his wife and child. I knew Shirley and Cindy wouldn't be much help. I went to a marine hardware store, asked around, and eventually found a twenty-three-year-old kid who wanted to go named Dave Davis, who we immediately began calling Dave Dave. Shirley and my then-fourteen-year-old daughter Cindy rounded out the crew.

We set sail right after the school year ended. We left from Alamitos Bay filled with high hopes, excitement, and yes, a few nerves.

Skipper's Log 6/18/78

Barometer pressure 30.00

Left slip at Alamitos Bay about 10:15 for Hilo, Hawaii. Family and friends came to see us off. Shirley, my wife, daughter Cindy, and crew member Dave Davis aboard. Winds about 20 kts. Motored past the east end of Catalina, wind increased to about 30 kts, 8-to-10 foot swells, wind chop. Cindy & Shirley seasick. I didn't feel too hot either. Dave OK. Dave and I put on foul weather gear. Boat awash, forward hatch leaking.

I'd put a little barbecue grill onboard and our plan was that we were going to make hamburgers our first night to celebrate the beginning of our voyage. We had everything ready when suddenly this strong wind came up and really started pounding us. Shirley and Cindy started to get seasick; they went down below where they proceeded to get as sick as dogs. What a start to the trip — we had a rough passage just to get to Catalina, twenty-six miles off shore. Somehow we finally got out past Catalina, between it and San Clemente Island, and I took a shot with the sextant so I could start charting our course. We never did have our hamburger feast because everyone was so sick; we had to throw the meat overboard the next day because it had spoiled.

Before we left, everybody kept saying to me, "Hey Art, you're going to Hawaii in June? It's a piece of cake!" Well, it wasn't a piece of cake! I couldn't use the stars to navigate because it was overcast the entire voyage. I tried to take sunshots during the day to plot our course, but sometimes all I could see was the highlight of the sun through the clouds. I knew how to shoot the stars, but I never had a chance to do it because I never could get three stars lined up to get a triangulation with my sextant. That summer these hurricanes called chabascos were coming out of Mexico heading straight for Hawaii, of course. Let me tell you, those things caused some storms! One night I was on watch and there were seven line squalls in a row. They call it a line squall because you can see the storm brewing on the horizon and then all of a sudden the wind will come up around fifty or sixty knots, and it will start raining like hell. Believe me, you don't know rain until you've been rained on at sea. It's like sitting under a pipe with a raging stream of water running on your head. On the mizzen-mast, right where the rain would hit it and run off, you could put a pail under the run-off, and a couple of seconds later it would be full.

During one storm, rain leaked into the front of our forward hatch because it wasn't sealed properly by Gary, my joiner guy. All of our sleeping bags and belongings up front got soaked — rain at sea is something else. There's no such things as individual raindrops, at least that I could distinguish, just solid sheets of water. At the time I had a full beard, and it would get wet and dry out, get wet and dry out; I would go down below and shake it and all the salt that had dried in it would fall out like a big salt shaker. I got so soaked with salt water on the trip that the fingernails on both of my hands lifted up halfway down, and got so raw I had trouble buttoning a button or zippering a zipper. It rained like that a lot of the way to Hawaii.

Skipper's Log

6/23/78

I still can't get another sun shot because of the overcast weather. I don't know where all the nice weather is in this part of the Pacific everyone tells you about. Before I left on this trip everyone I spoke with would say, "Wait until you get into the trades, you'll love it!" I'm still waiting.

One night we were in a terrible storm, the wind was blowing like hell and we were in a following sea — the water would swell about six inches from coming in the stern before falling away. Needless to say, if the water started spilling over into the stern, we would have a big problem — such as possibly going under. I had just a little jib up as well as the mizzen. To keep from being blown over, we dropped the staysail and the main. I had two forty-five-pound CQR anchors on each side of the bowsprit and 450 feet of 3/8 chain up in the chain locker in the bow, and that chain weighed over a pound per foot, so you can imagine how much weight was up there. We were screaming along — now every boat has a hull speed—and the hull speed of my boat was seven knots. If you exceed hull speed, as you get going faster and faster, the boat sinks lower and lower in the water. The faster you go, the lower you sink and I only had about eighteen inches of freeboard to begin with. Not a lot of margin for error. Despite my efforts to slow down, I was doing between 8 ¾ and 9 knots, and I was worried that if that bow went under we'd be in big trouble. When you realize that a cubic yard of water weighs almost a ton, you can see the kind of trouble we'd be in. If the driving of our forward momentum hit the bow and the bow went under, our boat would pitch-pole end over end. I went up to the bow life-line attached, and watched and watched, but thank God it never did dip. Even if we had, I tell myself now, that boat had 7000 pounds of lead in the keel and was designed in such a way that we could go end over end or roll and it would come right side up. I'm just glad I never had the chance to find out whether or not that was really true!

It was very important to me that we maintain a diligent schedule of keeping watch during the night. You can't ever take anything at sea for granted; even a momentary lapse could cost you your life. I did worry about crossing freighter lanes. They're clearly marked on your charts, but as you're sailing, you don't know exactly where you are, so you never know when you're going to run into them. That's why I wanted to have a twenty-four-hour watch, although Dave Dave didn't take watch as seriously as I did.

One night I came up to take watch about two in the morning, and the cockpit was totally empty. It was like a knife to my stomach. My only thought was, *My God, he went overboard!"* It was very upsetting. I really got emotional; I was truly afraid that the poor guy had drowned. I frantically looked everywhere for him. At night on the ocean it's completely pitch black, especially when it's overcast; there's no moon, no stars. Finally I made it up to the bow, and there he was, right by where the anchor was stowed, sound asleep. Thank God he was alive — but that didn't take away the fact that he scared the shit outta me.

Another night, it was pouring rain and I went up to take a watch and Dave was, once again, fast asleep. He had on storm gear, those yellow slickers you always see sailors in, and he was sleeping on top of the cabin. The water was running off the sail down his neck, down inside the arm of the slicker, out the end of the sleeve, and he slept through the whole thing. That's who Dave was. He was twenty-three. Kids think they are immortal; they don't worry about danger. Me — I was concerned about getting run over by a freighter.

One night I got up to take watch when I saw that there was friggin' water on the cabin sole! *Sonofabitch,* I said to myself, *what is that?* We were motor-sailing because it was dead calm, so I opened up the engine room door and saw the flywheel on the engine spinning around and the whole thing was churning up with suds, looking like a big washing machine. I thought, *What the hell is going on; water's coming in!* I first tried the pump on the engine, but it wouldn't engage. I grabbed the handle on a twenty-five-gallon hand-pump, and started pumping by hand.

Shirley woke up, saw me, and yelled, "Are we sinking?"

I said, "No goddamit, we're not sinking," but she wasn't convinced.

She started to panic. "Cindy, Cindy you better get dressed. We might be sinking!"

Skipper's Log

6/30/78

I panicked, opened the engine room door. The engine was running and partially submerged. I threw the clutch on the Jobsco pump-in, but it didn't seem to work. So I started

pumping the Whale 25. I thought that pump was too hard to
pump, but it sure went like hell this morning.

Well, I pumped and finally got the water down in the bilge and found
a stream of water smaller than my pinky going into the bilge from a hole
in an Aqualift tank used to cool the engine. I hung upside down into the
bilge, and found this little bronze plug that had popped out. Electrolysis
had taken the threads off of it and it had fallen out. Luckily there were
still enough threads for it to hold, so I screwed it back in and stopped the
flood. I didn't even know that plug was there until that happened. The suds
were from a bottle of Prell shampoo that had leaked into the bilge. One
of the two alternators I had was flooded, and the starter got some water
in it, but everything worked okay. The entire rest of the trip, every time
I needed to start the engine to charge the batteries, I crossed my fingers
because the water had flooded one alternator, but it worked every time.
But that was one scary night. I started to have trouble just before I came
into Long Beach. I had to decompress two cylinders on the diesel to start
it. Eventually I had to buy a new alternator and starter.

Along the way we lost our starboard shroud off of the main. It was nicro
pressed, which is a process you use to hold the cables together. Apparently
the nicro presses on the shroud worked and worked against each other until
the cable just broke. Fortunately I'd brought an extra halyard, so I tied
it down to the starboard side and it held all the way to Hawaii. I learned
my lessons about nicro presses, and when we got to Hawaii we changed
everything to airplane fittings with bolts, except for the mizzen.

We didn't see a lot of sea life, or freighters for that matter, after we left
Catalina. A lot of little flying fish wound up on our deck from the waves
crashing over us. They weren't very big, certainly not big enough to eat.
I have a picture taken a thousand miles out of an albatross following us.
Albatrosses spend all of their time out on the ocean and never go to land
except when they're mating, but this one was trying to land on our gaff.
He must have had a six-foot wingspan.

I wasn't much of fisherman before the trip — we brought fishing
equipment along with us, thinking maybe we could catch something
and have something fresh to eat — but Dave Dave never did any fishing.
Bringing the stuff was his idea; I was too busy with the navigation, trying
to shoot the sun and stay on course and run the boat. With all the storms
we had, I had my hands full. We didn't see any fish or whales or sharks

after we left San Clemente Island. We didn't get to do any fishing. The sunrises and sunsets we saw when it wasn't overcast were beautiful.

It's funny the thoughts that go through your head when you're out in the middle of the ocean at night and it's pitch black. When you're down below, water can hit the side of the hull and it sounds like someone is banging on it with a sledge hammer. You come rushing out topside to see; did the mast fall down, the rigging, what happened? And it's nothing; out there everything just sounds different. It gets so dark at night you can't see the bow of the boat; you can't see several feet ahead of you. You start to imagine all kinds of things out there, because you hear sounds that the ocean's making and sometimes you imagine you see something out in the water, but there's nothing there. And that went on every night. Even though I knew it, my imagination would make up stuff.

At the time of our voyage, the Cold War was still going on. One night I was by myself and I started thinking, *What if there's an atomic war while we are out here and we don't know about it, and when we get to Hawaii there's no one there?* That really got to me. Sometimes I'd go to sleep — I never slept a whole night through, two hours at a time maybe — but I'd wake up and look down at the water and think, *Shit, this doesn't look any different from yesterday — did we go anywhere?!* Of course we had, we just didn't have any frame of reference. Like I say, when you're all alone, all kinds of crazy things go through your head.

I was very concerned with conserving our fresh drinking water because even though we had eighty gallons, we had no idea how long we'd be out there. Because of this, I only let the people wash in salt water. I'd just sit on deck and wash myself with cold ocean water, but for Shirley and Cindy I had these little plastic solar bags for warm water. I'd lay them on the deck, fill 'em with water and the sun would heat 'em up, and that's what they'd use for a warm shower. I only allowed fresh water to be used for brushing teeth and drinking.

Shirley didn't eat a lot of stuff on the voyage because she's gluten-intolerant. I'd brought along stuff that wouldn't spoil: Cup O' Soup, noodles, canned beef stew. In addition to not having a lot of food she could eat, the poor woman was seasick for a week after we left. She spent the whole time in her bunk down below, feeling like crap. One day, God bless her, she got up and said, "I'm gonna make you guys a great breakfast — bacon, eggs, everything." Well, after she'd been in the bunk for a whole week she was pretty wobbly and we were in rough seas anyway; she got out of the bunk — the boat was pitching back and forth — and whacked her head on one cap rail. The boat swung the other way, and she whacked her head on the other one … and in two seconds, she was back in the bunk, almost unconscious.

Skipper's Log

6/24/78

She got out of her bunk and immediately bounced from one side of the cabin to the other, hit her head, and fell into the dinette. I thought she had a brain concussion, but she was okay except for a bump on the back of her head. She proceeded to make breakfast after I lit the stove and handed her everything she needed. She looked like an octopus trying to hold everything in her hands because the boat was rocking and nothing would stay where she put it. I have never heard her cuss that much in the 28 years we've been married.

But she'd done it. She was determined to make us breakfast!

I don't know exactly what my beliefs are when it comes to religion, but one incident during our trip almost seemed like divine intervention. We had been at sea for quite a while, a couple of weeks, and I knew I was too far north. The Hawaiian Islands, like Kauai and Oahu, are a hundred miles apart. You could sail right between them and never know it, and I was pretty damn sure that's exactly what was happening. What I couldn't figure out was why. My sunshots and my running fix on my charts were not coinciding; I knew they were getting farther and farther apart and I couldn't figure it out. I knew from my class that if you take a sunshot when your chronometer hits exact noon, you'll find out what latitude you're on, and I knew that would at least give me some idea of where the hell I was. It's very difficult to take a sunshot of any kind on a boat that's moving every direction. You gotta hold that sextant so precise and bring that sun ball exactly on the horizon, and when it is, you say "mark" and someone tells you the exact time and then you do your calculations. I was trying to do this — and I was not having any luck. I was really worried that we were so far off course we were gonna be in real trouble, when suddenly Shirley yelled, "Artie, Artie, there's a boat over there!" Honest to God, it was the first vessel we'd seen in two weeks.

Skipper's Log

7/3/78

I got on my radio and called for any ship in the area to answer. Please! One answered and gave us our exact position. I still can't figure out how our DRs were so off. Right now we're heading to Maui instead of Hilo.

I was right; I was way too far north. But I still didn't know why. I checked the compasses to see if maybe something was in the way and throwing the magnetism off, but that wasn't it. I was stumped. And then that night it hit me. I was dozing off, in the alpha state when you're still sort of half-awake, and all of a sudden it friggin' occurred to me. I had made a simple mistake in subtraction and addition on the compass deviation and that was what threw us off. I corrected it, and sure enough, that was the mistake. On the way home I said, "Well, at least I'm not stupid enough to miss all of North and South America!"

Skipper's Log

7/5/78

Today I finally felt like reading. Shirley put "La Boheme" on the tape deck and we spent a very relaxing afternoon. I took a nap about 1500, got up about 1700 and took a sun shot. My navigation is right on the money now. What a relief. About 600 miles from Maui now.

Since we'd lost a couple of days, I changed my course to Lahaina on Maui. We were all excited to finally be getting close to our destination.

Skipper's Log

7/9/78

Winds have kept up all day, haven't had to touch the sails (that's a novelty). Turned on the VHF, I figured we were about 140 miles out and much to my surprise, the Hawaii weather station came in. I then turned on my RDF and pulled in all sorts of AM stations from Hawaii. Shirley was so thrilled to hear a radio playing again. Cindy is listening to some music now.

-Several hours later-

*Well we just finished our third rain squall for today. I'm still
waiting for that beautiful, balmy trade wind weather.*

I'll never forget the excitement when we first spotted the Hawaiian
Islands. Lahaina is up from the smaller island of Molokai, which years
ago used to be a leper colony. I saw a navigation light off Molokai, but
instead of heading up, I headed right for that light because I was so excited.
Unfortunately, we ended up in the channel between Molokai and Maui
and sure enough, this strong wind started blowing right up against us.
Because it was a headwind, we had no choice but to kick on the engine
and motor sail. So close to the end! I always revved the engine at about
1600 rpm, but because of this headwind it didn't look like we were going
anywhere. I thought, *Shit, this engine can do better than that,"* so I put it up
to 1900 rpm, and what do you know, we started making headway. Shirley,
Cindy, and Dave Dave were all down below, and I was up in the cockpit.
I had my safety harness on, but maybe because I was excited about seeing
land so close, I didn't have it hooked up. All of a sudden a huge wave came
at us off the port bow. Sonofabitch! I decided to head up into it, but as we
did, the boat slid off the wave and fell sideways into the trough and the
boom from the main hit the water. I was immediately thrown out of the
cockpit and the boom from the mizzen swung and caught me in the head,
giving me a pretty nasty cut in the process. At this point, the boat righted
itself up and we kept going. I don't know what they were doing down
below, but Dave Dave pushed open the hatch and said matter-of-factly,
"Hey Art, your head's bleeding."

I just looked at him and said, "I know my head's bleeding, goddammit!"
Then all of a sudden smoke came pouring out of the engine room — it was
on fire! As it turned out, the electrical harness was on the door of the engine
room, something vibrated and caused some insulation to come off the wire
and it was no big deal. I taped everything up and we made our triumphant
approach into Lahaina. With one more adventure yet to come …

Chapter Nineteen

We were coming into Lahaina at the exact same time there was a San Francisco-to-Lahaina single-handed race — and guess where the finish line was. We were coming in with a band playing, "When the Saints Come Marching In"; all these people were cheering and they saw me and said, "You're not one of the racers!"

They started to boo us and I said, "What did I do wrong?" I guess we were a strange sight compared to those racing yachts. We were twenty-two and-a-half days at sea and I think we finally saw the light on Molokai about the twenty-first day.

When we finally anchored, we were so beat we just wanted to go out and get something to eat, because we weren't about to be cooking on the boat after all that. After you get off a boat, you can't walk a straight line.

Skipper's Log

7/11/78

> *We got off the boat for the first time in over 23 days and all walked like we were drunk. The strangest feeling. Shirl wanted to stay on shore but we couldn't find a place so back on the boat, but it was so calm. We all slept soundly.*

My son Jeff and his wife came to see us the next day and as soon as they saw us, they laughed hysterically. Cindy's long hair was so completely tangled that she and my wife had to take a buck knife and cut the knots out. Shirley had lost twenty pounds; her jeans wouldn't stay up.

We stayed in Hawaii for three weeks, exploring and driving around, but we still slept on the boat. We had a lot of fun; Lahaina wasn't as touristy then as it is now. One day, Shirley and Cindy were sitting on the beach and some guys asked them if they wanted to buy some 'shrooms. In those days, lots of guys were out there selling pot and stuff. Even though Cindy was only fourteen, she went into bars and they served her Piña Coladas.

Jeff and I went out sailing one day, but there was a hurricane still following us in from Mexico. Because the storm was blowing in, the harbor master told us we had to go out into the harbor off-shore because it wasn't safe to anchor. We had to put both CQRs out at forty-five degrees from each other, and put the danforth anchor out from the stern to wait out the hurricane. Fortunately, it didn't get too bad where we were.

After Lahaina we sailed over to Honolulu and Dave Dave slept on the boat, while Shirley and I got a hotel room. We got new fittings put on the boat and rented a car to do some more exploring. We drove all over and saw lots of interesting stuff. We saw a program that featured traditional Hawaiian ceremonies and boats, went swimming in these streams, and dove off rocks. Shirley and I knew some people from Seal Beach who had a home over in Kauai by this beautiful beach, so we took a little two-engine plane over to see them. We had to load it from the front backward because if we loaded the back of the plane first, it would tip up on its tail.

As we were walking down the street one afternoon in Kauai, this guy yelled, "Hey, Art!" I looked around and saw the coach from Fountain Valley, so I went over and visited with him for a while. We went out into Hanalei Bay and were the only two people on the whole beach. We drove around and visited the Fern Grotto and a bunch of other places, sightseeing, then flew back to Honolulu, and got ready for the return voyage home.

Chapter Twenty

In Honolulu, I put a notice up to hire some people to help me sail the "Sarah Ann" home and stand watch, because there was *no* way Shirley and Cindy were going to sail back; they were gonna fly home. Even I was very, very depressed, because I did NOT want to sail back either, but I had no choice — either sail the boat back or leave it there and try to sell it. I found a couple of girls who had sailed to Hawaii with their father who I should have taken, but there were two guys I had interviewed before them and I'd already promised them the job. Joe was about sixteen; Errol was eighteen and on his way to the University of Colorado in Boulder. The girls knew sailing, they knew their business. Joe and Errol had never been on a boat and didn't know anything about sailing. They were not prepared; they didn't even have raincoats. I should've listened to my gut and hired the girls anyway, but I'd already made a deal and figured how bad could it be? I got my answer soon enough. I signed them on and charged them three bucks a day to cover their food. Even then, one of them stiffed me when we got back.

From the moment we left Honolulu, I was dreading the trip back. For one, it's longer going back. The summer we left, we had to sail a thousand miles north before we could start heading east and pick up the winds off the Pacific High. A Marconi rig can point thirty degrees into the wind; my gaff rigger could point maybe forty-five. I had all these sailboats passing me on the starboard side, cutting into the wind and I had to do it the hard way. From almost the first minute, Joe and his buddy were a disaster; they just drove me crazy. We were leaving Honolulu and Joe saw some bubbles coming up in the water and he said, "Hey Art, what are those bubbles?"

I said, "how the frig do I know?"

Whenever a boat would go by I'd hear, "Hey, Art, where are they going?"

I'd just look at them and say, "How the hell do I know where they're going?!!" These are the questions they asked me.

I offered to help them to learn how to sail — nothing. And then they started leaving their stuff all over the cockpit. It was more than just an annoyance; if stuff gets caught in the rigging when you're hauling up a line, and someone's underwear goes up, it gets caught in the blocks and could be big, big trouble. I told them, "You leave anything in that cockpit that gets in the way and it's going overboard!" They didn't believe me, so their stuff started disappearing. Finally they got the message. They didn't care about standing watch. Even when they stayed awake, they did it half-heartedly.

Skipper's Log

8/1/78

Dave and I have been taking the night watches and Joe and Errol the day watches. They don't have enough warm clothes to keep warm at night, especially for their feet. I lent them each a set of foul weather gear, but I don't have boots and other clothes for them. They really came equipped. They are both so naïve I can't believe it. I decided to take a bath on deck and Joe asked if he could; I said I didn't care. He moved right in on me and wanted to do it then and there! Joe is very demanding and pushy and I'm a little bit uptight about getting home, I guess.

One day I was in the cockpit and all of a sudden the mizzen mast fell down on me. I yelled, "Joe, Joe!" who was down below.

He called up very casually, "What do you want, Art?"

I yelled back, "What do I want? Get your ass up here *now*; I need you *now*!" We hoisted up the mizzen mast with the halyard, tied it up, took the gaff and the sail and the boom off and tied them to the railings on the side and sailed without it. The mizzen doesn't give you a lot of power forward; it's more of a balancing sail. It's the jenny and the jib and the main that give you the power to sail.

Later we were sailing along and we were gonna eat dinner and it was Joe's turn to take watch. He was up there and started in with, "Hey, Art, how come I have to stay up here? How come I can't come down and eat with you?"

And I said, "Because it's your turn to watch. Watch means watch; see if anything is coming."

Errol, Dave Dave, and I were eating, when all of a sudden Joe casually said, "Hey Art, I think there's a boat coming."

I jumped topside — and there was a friggin' freighter bearing right down on us! Holy shit. The problem is lots of times freighters don't even have their radar on, so they might not have even known we were there. As fast I could, I turned on the radio — nothing. The mast that had fallen had my radio antenna on top, and I thought it was damaged so there was no way the freighter captain could hear me. I looked up, and this monster was coming right at us. If a ship that size hit a boat our size, it literally would be like a bug on the windshield; they wouldn't even know they'd hit anything. I shouted into the radio, "This is the Sarah Ann. I have red sails. I'm off your port bow; do you see me?" I gave 'em my call letters and everything. "I say, do you see me, do you see me?" Well, it took a while before someone got up and took a look, but finally they saw me. The freighter fell off the starboard and I fell off the port, and we passed each other by what wasn't more than a couple of hundred feet. You could count the rivets on the freighter as it went by. That's how close we came to getting run over.

Shirley and Me

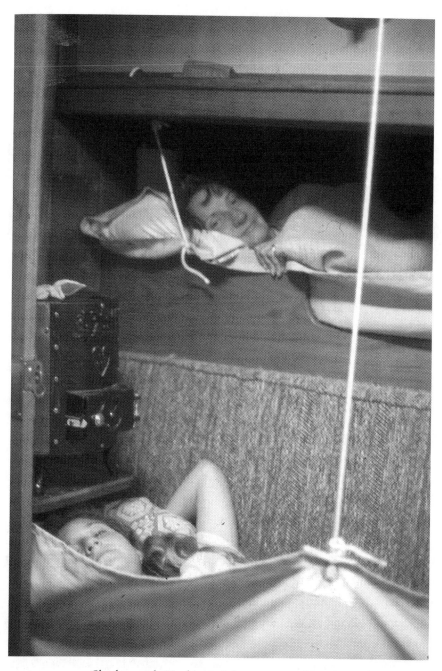

Shirley and Cindy seasick on way to Hawaii

The Sarah Ann

New House

My Family

Fire Destruction

Chapter Twenty-One

Thankfully, after almost being crushed by a freighter, the rest of the voyage home was fairly routine.

Skipper's Log

8/6/78

The weather is just beautiful today and has been really great since we left Hawaii. Shirley, you wouldn't believe how nice it's been; sunny, warm, calm seas. No storms, and very little if any sail changes.

We finally got the thousand miles north we needed to and were able to head east. Back in those days, Japanese fishermen used big glass balls to float their nets. One day I saw one bobbing loose in the water, turned around, and picked it up. It had a whole colony of sea life attached to it: mussels, barnacles, shrimp, and crabs. I knocked them all off, put it in a garbage bag, and brought it home. By the time we got back the stink was unbelievable. I had it for years and years until it was finally lost it in the fire.

We saw dolphins — they like to ride your bow wake — flipping up in front, and close to shore we saw some small pilot whales.

Skipper's Log

8/23/78

About 0530 this morning there must have been a hundred or more porpoises playing back and forth across our bow. It was really great to watch them. It's the first real sign of sea life we've seen up close this entire trip. Other than that, the only thing that interests me is the wind because <u>I want to get home!</u>

Joe and Errol continued to be useless. The eighteen-year-old was constipated for thirteen days. I'd never heard of anybody being backed up for that long. Well, one morning I was going to use the head and I saw these really strange-looking turds in there, like little hard, brown golf balls. I thought, *oh my God.* I tried to flush, tried to flush, but they wouldn't go down. I finally had to reach in with toilet paper and pick these things out and throw them overboard. I knew who was responsible, so I thought about sticking them under his nose while he was asleep, but I wasn't that cruel. But I thought about it.

There weren't that many storms on the way home. We didn't have the mizzen mast, but the winds were coming out of the east then so we were fine. When we got about eight hundred miles off the mainland coast we were way down by friggin' Ensenada in Mexico, several hundred miles south of where we wanted to be. I had to tack so that we could come back up north again. I can't tell you how glad I was to finally be back. After what seemed like forever, suddenly the Channel Islands appeared on the horizon, which meant we were almost home. I started sailing toward San Nicolas Island when all of a sudden a Coast Guard plane came flying over, tipping his wings back and forth which meant "get on the horn!" I couldn't figure out what the hell was going on.

I got on the radio and the pilot said, "Skipper, you are sailing into a missile firing range!"

I though, *Holy shit, all this way and we're gonna get hit by a missile?* No sooner were the words out of his mouth than three big warships came up over the horizon and I thought, *Holy shit, we are in trouble for sure!*

The pilot said, "Can you change course to such-and such-heading"?

I'd been out there for twenty-four days now, so I got pissed and answered back, "I'm in a sailboat. I can't change course; I can't motor here and there." Part of the reason I was mad was because the starter had gotten wet and wasn't working too well, so I radioed Vandenburg Air Force Base and explained my situation.

The dispatcher said, "Can you at least change your course to 100 degrees east?"

Well I had just done that anyway, so I said, "Yeah, I think I could handle that." I changed course, and no missiles were fired overhead, but it sure was scary as hell.

When we got in past San Nicolas Island, I decompressed the cylinders and finally got the engine started. Halfway home we met a freighter and I got to talking to the captain on the radio, who said he was heading into Long Beach, too. I said, "Could you do me a favor and call my wife and tell her you saw me out here?" And he did. He phoned her and told her he'd met her husband out at sea and he was okay; he was sailing home.

And that was our trip to Hawaii. It took us 22 ½ days going, we stayed three weeks, and it took us 26 ½ days coming home. It was a trip I'll never, never forget, easily the most exciting thing I've done in my life. You don't know what blue water sailing is until you're out in it and you hit thirty-foot seas and you're down in the troughs; you can't see the horizon because there's water all around you. It's just unreal. I'm grateful I had the opportunity to do it.

After we returned, I learned from my cousin Eric that while sitting in the East Village in New York one day he noticed someone walking by wearing a t-shirt with a picture of the "Sarah Ann' on it. Eric ran after the guy and asked him where he got it. He replied, "From the owner. I hitched a ride back from Hawaii to California with him." What are the odds?!

My son Jeff and I continued to sail the Channel Islands after I got back from Hawaii. We visited Avalon, the only city on Santa Catalina Island, many times. For those of you who have no knowledge about Catalina, it is a rocky island located twenty-two miles southwest of Los Angeles. It is twenty-two miles long and eight miles across at its widest point. The highest point is Mt. Orizabo at 2097 feet, and today around 3700 call Catalina home. There's quite a bit of indigenous wildlife including foxes, bald eagles, and about 150 American bison, the descendants of fifteen bison brought over for a movie shoot in 1924 and left there.

One weekend in the summer of 1981, Jeff and I sailed to Avalon to experience their annual chili cook-off. I don't know how long this event had been going on, but it seemed to grow more elaborate every year to the point where 10,000 tourists invaded the small town. Every room was booked, the harbor was packed, and people were sleeping outside on grassy areas on the perimeter of the cook-off event, located just north of the casino (a round, two-story Art Deco dance hall built by William Wrigley in the 1920s to attract tourists). Today there's a movie theater downstairs and a dance hall upstairs, and it is a famous landmark very much prized by the locals. Besides chili tasting, there were many different brands of beer, tequila, and other spirits available as well as a stage featuring live music and other entertainment. The event I remember most was the wet t-shirt contest. Can you picture the scene? Guys in the crowd with high-powered squirt guns aimed at the women onstage, squirting as fast as they could. Everyone was drinking, and many were drunk — including the contestants who began taking off their t-shirts. It got pretty wild and some people got so carried away they started having sex in public. One couple was performing on the main streets of Avalon! The party continued long into the night and Jeff and I ended up on a fairly large yacht owned by an attorney from Newport Beach who spent the evening standing in front of the main salon smoking a joint and reciting poetry. The party lasted into Sunday and was the wildest debauchery I've ever seen. Someone vandalized the casino, and that was the last straw. That year ended up being the last great chili cook-off in Avalon. There were other incidents that I vaguely recall, but I don't want to incriminate anyone, so you'll just have to use your imagination as to just how wild the partying really got. Sailing can be a lot of fun!

I kept the Sarah Ann for a while when we got back, put in a new starter and alternator because of the salt water that had flooded the engine room. There's a lot of maintenance on a boat, a lot of varnishing, just a lot of work. About this time, my son started his family and had children and couldn't help out as much, so in 1981 I sold her and bought a three-quarter keel Marconi-rig fiberglass boat from Bristol, Rhode Island. It was a smaller boat, easier to take care of, easier to sail — one person could sail it. I had about $75,000 into the Sarah Ann, which was a lot of money in those days. I sold one of the anchors, the life raft, and a couple of other things separately, and sold the boat itself for $65,000. I paid $30,000 for the new boat and with the left-over cash I bought Shirley a new car.

Oh, I almost forgot to tell you — when we finally got back from Hawaii I was two days late coming back to school for the fall semester and the principal started to give me a hard time. I just said, "just chalk it up to seasick time!"

Chapter Twenty-Two

See as much of the world as you possibly can. You will never be sorry.

The voyage to Hawaii was just one of my many travels. During my time at Lincoln, I made three different trips to Europe with the Foreign Study League. For the first two I was in charge of ten or twelve kids; on the third trip I was in charge of the whole tour. We hit all the places you'd want to see: Rome, Capri, Firenze, Bern, Munich, England. The first time I ever saw *Fiddler on the Roof* was in a West End Theater in London. It was very touching for me to see because the whole story reflects the world that my parents came from in Europe. We also saw *The Man in the Glass Booth*, stayed in castles, saw museums, really had a ball. And of course, I had a couple of adventures that weren't exactly in the tour brochure.

On the trip we took in 1969, I happened to be in the Netherlands the day that the astronauts were scheduled to land on the moon. I had to fly on ahead of the rest of the group to arrange for our accommodations in a dormitory in a city called Newbern. It happened to be some kind of national holiday there. I stopped into a bar that was three deep with people drinking beer.

After a few minutes, a guy tapped me on the shoulder and said, "You're an American, aren't you?"

I said, "Yeah, how do you know?"

He knew because another guy had seen me coming in on the train from Amsterdam and told him. They said, "You know, after this place closes we're going to this bar by the airport; do you want to come with us?" They were nice guys, and had a nice-looking blonde lady with them, so we all went to have a good time. Things started to wind down and we headed back; soon he was dropping everyone off except me.

I looked at my watch and said, "God, I really want to see the astronauts land."

He said, "No problem, we'll go to my place."

That was fine with me because I really didn't want to miss seeing this historical moment. I was really beat and I'd had all that beer. So when he asked me, "Do you want a drink? Do you want a Scotch?" I should have said, "No, I really shouldn't; I'm gonna fall asleep," but to be polite, I had a Scotch. Sure enough I fell asleep, and the next thing I knew, I felt something. I jumped up, my pants were around my ankles and my head was inside a big globe fixture hanging from the ceiling. (If you've ever been in the old-fashioned houses in Holland, you know the ceilings are very low.) I was thinking, *What the frig's going on?* The guy on the couch had his hands up over his face like I was gonna hit him. He had my belt unbuckled, my zipper unzipped, and I don't think he was thinking about watching the moon landing.

I said, "I'm not gonna hit you; just take me back to the dorm. I wanna see the astronauts land." We went back to the dorm, and I sat with the people who worked at the Dutch school and we watched the first men land on the moon.

On another trip, we were in Italy and some of the other adult chaperones and I were in my room and we decided to have martinis. I had a bottle of gin and made the drinks; everyone started drinking and then they all said, "What's the matter with these drinks; they taste like water!" We checked the bottle — it seems that the kids had come into our room, poured out all the gin and filled the bottles with water!

Another night we decided to go out to eat, so I picked a Russian restaurant that I later found out was run by Russian Jews. I looked at the menu and started talking to the waiter, speaking Yiddish with each other. All the counselors were surprised; they thought I was speaking Russian because they didn't know one language from another — they had no idea I spoke Yiddish. They didn't realize that Yiddish is a universal language, the only language without a country. You could probably go to China and run into Jews who speak Yiddish. After a while, the waiter returned with a big pitcher filled to the brim, frosted on the outside, and started filling all the water glasses. We picked up the glasses and took a drink — it was straight vodka! It was a tradition with these Russian Jews to serve it to their guests.

On one visit to Rome, our tour stayed in a convent. I had a private room on the second floor, and was told the nuns locked the front door at 11 p.m. sharp. There was no other way to get in or out and they wouldn't allow anyone else to have a key, including me, and I was in charge of the tour! After touring all day visiting churches, art galleries, museums, and historical sights, I liked to have some fun and let off steam in the evening. I had a window that looked onto a roof and from there to a trellis which led down to the street level. I decided that was the way I was going to come and go after hours. Soon enough, all the counselors found out my secret and after that there was a stream of people coming in and out of my window each night. Out in the street, Italian men gave me the high sign and congratulations, saying something in Italian I didn't understand, but it seemed to indicate that I was cool. This went on for a while so I finally asked our Italian bus driver why I was getting so much attention. He explained that they thought I was quite a stud muffin and lover having all these women coming up to my room. Obviously at night they could see from the street and their apartment windows. What can I say, Italian men are very romantic.

Chapter Twenty-Three

*If you're unhappy with your current career or job, pick a new one!
It's never too late to start something new.*

I've had an incredible assortment of jobs in my life. I've picked apples in Connecticut, driven a taxi in Des Moines, stocked shelves at a wholesale grocery warehouse, operated a tractor on an Iowa farm pulling a harrow, waited tables at Wimpy's Steakhouse, sold life insurance, pots and pans, women's shoes, encyclopedias, Saturns and Subarus. Once on a farm in Iowa, I helped castrate pigs. They would take a pig, hold it down, cut open the scrotum, and take the testicles out. I think they put turpentine on the wound to seal it up, to keep it from bleeding. My job was to collect the testicles, and afterward, they had a big luncheon where they ate them; they called them Rocky Mountain Oysters. I didn't participate. Call me crazy but eating pigs' testicles somehow didn't appeal to me.

But of all the jobs I've had, I've had the most fun with my most recent one — acting.

When I was in high school, I had the lead in three high school plays. It wasn't that I had a lot of skill or was that confident or anything else, it was just that I didn't have a lot of competition because no one else volunteered. In those days a lot of kids, especially in a town that wasn't that sophisticated, thought acting was gay. If you were macho, you just didn't do it. At the high school we had a rickety old stage. It made noise when you walked on it; you could practically feel the whole stage moving. There was no sound system and the lighting was very amateurish.

Shirley and I acted together in a play when we first got married. It was at the Moodus Theater and was sponsored by the Sisterhood of the

Jewish Community. Even though I'd had some experience, I never really thought of acting as something I would pursue professionally. But one day that all changed.

I really wasn't thinking about giving up counseling at Fountain Valley High when I walked into the school cafeteria. I didn't usually go into the cafeteria; I used to bring crackers and cheese and fruit for lunch, but this one day I forgot to bring anything. At the time, I had a full beard and Carol Cooney, the dramatic coach, who was putting on the musical, *Bye, Bye Birdie*, yelled,"Art, Art, Art! We need some older people to be the drunken Shriners."

I said, "Carol, I don't want to do that."

She wouldn't give up. "Oh, come on, you don't have any lines or anything; all you have to do is dance."

I said, "Dance? That's even worse! I can't dance!" Finally to get rid of her, I said okay. Then I was up onstage in *Bye, Bye Birdie* and everything changed. I discovered this excitement and adrenaline that pumped into my system, and I formed a relationship with the audience — all this and I didn't even have any lines!

At that time of the year we were registering eighth-graders for the next year's freshman class and I got friendly with one of the parents. I said, "Hey, did you see our production of *Bye Bye Birdie?*" She said no. I told her I was in it, and then joked, "Maybe I'll go on to become a movie star."

She laughed and said, "Well, if you're really interested, there's a class going on down at this place called the South Coast Actors' Studio. A Huntington Beach policeman I know is taking classes there and he says it's legitimate." So I checked it out.

The acting coach there, Al Valletta, was teaching cold reading classes, where you take a script and try to act it out without memorizing it. I liked what I saw, so I signed up for one of his classes. Al was a very low-key guy and tried to be nice; he didn't want to say anything mean to anybody to upset or insult them, but after I did my first scene, he looked at me for a moment and finally said, "Art, you're really terrible." He didn't realize who he was talking to because I'm not the kind of guy who gives up on something because someone tells me I can't do it.

I said, "I'm gonna make it, do it right, and succeed." And Al must have seen something he liked, because he took me under his wing. We did a lot of improvs, where he helped me learn to bring out my emotions. When you're a man of fifty, it's more difficult than for a younger person who doesn't have all these "no's" and "don'ts" and restrictions in his head.

As you get older you're accomplished, you're successful in a career … you don't want to look foolish in front of your peers. There's also all that garbage about how men aren't supposed to cry, they're not supposed to show emotion. Al just said, "Forget all that stuff! This is an acting class and you don't intellectualize the parts. Everything in acting is visceral; it comes from your gut." I took his advice and finally became very emotional. In fact, as I took more classes he started to call me the "crybaby."

What really brought me out was an acting seminar Al started up in Lake Arrowhead. In fact, that's how Shirley and I got the idea to come up and look for a lot to build on up there. She would come up for the seminars and do the cooking. We'd come up on a Friday night, maybe twelve, fourteen actors — and spend the whole weekend totally immersed. People didn't even want to go to bed because they got so wound up and excited about the acting. We'd get up in the morning, eat breakfast, and then Al would give out scenes, monologues, and then we'd do more improvs. We grew more in one weekend than we would in months of classes down the hill. It would get pretty intense. He'd have an improv where he'd tell us we were all on a boat and then he'd give everyone a relationship to each other, father or husband or boyfriend … and then he'd say, "This boat is sinking and there's no way any of you are going to get rescued. What do you do, what do you say, what is your relationship with the people you care about? How do you react, what do you think about, what do you talk about with your father or your wife or your fiancée or even a stranger?" It was very powerful and incredibly helpful for me in developing my skills.

During another improv, I was a murderer on death row, and other people played my visitors. One would be the wife of the victim, another would be the daughter of the victim, another one his brother, my wife, my attorney, or the prosecuting attorney. These sessions really brought out our emotions, and that's how I really got interested in acting. What gave me satisfaction as an actor was that I could experience the complete range of emotions and when it was over, return to reality. I experienced it, but I didn't have to live it. It was all make believe.

One thing acting has done for sure is make me kind of a crybaby. I even cry at Hallmark commercials. Acting for me is being able to express myself, any emotion I want. I did a scene recently in a Hallmark film called *Healing Hands,* but there were no directions in the script suggesting how I was supposed to play the scene. In the story the lead character had inherited an ability to heal people. In my scene, my character wants him to fix my hand because it is completely crippled with rheumatoid arthritis. After the take, I said to the director, "I hope that wasn't too emotional."

He said, "Art, this is a Hallmark film; get as emotional as you want."

In the next take I got more emotional and as soon as we were done, the leading lady came up to me and said, "You made me cry!"

The director said, "Art, you really nailed it; you did a great job." And that's the fun of acting, that I'm still getting compliments at my age.

But back in the beginning, I had no idea how to get an agent or make any money acting, but people started saying to me, "Art, you should join AFTRA," the American Federation of Television and Radio Artists. If you join AFTRA and get an AFTRA part with lines, then you are eligible to join the Screen Actors Guild or SAG. Without that, getting into SAG is a real Catch-22 — you can't get SAG parts without being in SAG and you can't get into SAG unless you've got a SAG part. But you can get into all these other unions, like AFTRA.

Around this time a woman in my area named Marion Berzon decided to start a theatrical agency and so in order to look like I was a professional, I joined AFTRA and lo and behold, Marion Berzon got me an audition. I had to do a scene for an assistant casting director from a soap opera called *General Hospital* who cast actors in roles that had less than five lines. It was very nerve-wracking, but the amazing thing is — I got the part. And just like that, I was on *General Hospital* and a year later I was eligible to join SAG, which I did in 1981, two years before I quit teaching to go into acting full-time.

From that point I got a lot of parts while still working at Fountain Valley — I'd just take sick days to go to auditions and jobs. It was about this time that Proposition 13 was passed in California, which took away all the funding from local property taxes from the schools and gave it to Sacramento. The schools were in dire need of money, so one day the superintendent fired the entire counseling staff. He told us, "If you want to work in the school system, you have to be a teacher."

I thought, *Fine, I didn't become a counselor because I didn't like teaching.* So I said, "I'm good at social studies, geography, history, government," and they stuck me teaching general math and record-keeping. That really blew my mind.

I went to the principal, who just said, "C'mon Art, anybody can teach math."

I said, "No, they can't, especially general math, because these kids are the weakest math students and they need a real proficient, expert math teacher who can help them out!" To add insult to injury, they didn't even give me textbooks, just old workbooks; I had to run off pages every day on an old mimeograph machine to stay ahead of the kids.

I was so pissed off — for two years I'd had a lot of money taken out for a tax shelter annuity to get a little money saved because I knew I'd lose a lot of retirement — but I stayed until June of 1983 and then quit. I was fifty-five-years-old and had twenty-eight years of experience but only twenty-three years in California, so when I retired I was only getting a thousand dollars a month retirement — not a lot of money to retire on. Shirley kept working to support us. I was hoping my acting career would take off, but it's a crazy business and you really never know if you're going to sink or swim.

In the fall of 1983 a new agent, a young kid who didn't know anything about the business (his mother financed his whole agency) got me an audition ... and I went and met Albert Brooks.

Chapter Twenty-Four

Albert Brooks was giving general interviews for parts in his upcoming movie, *Lost in America*. He was the writer, the director, the star — everything in this film. I interviewed with him and it went pretty well, and in January of 1984 he called me back to cold read a scene with him in the role of an employment counselor. I read the scene sitting across a desk from him and when we finished, he said, "Good job, Art."

Being a new actor, not knowing the protocol, I replied, "So does that mean I have the part?"

He got all flustered and said, "God, no one ever asked me that before," but didn't really answer. I figured "what the heck" and walked out the door. He came running out after me and said, "Hey, Art, come on back." We sat down on the couch and talked. I picked up that he was nervous about me being a fairly new actor and was worried that I might freak out in front of the cameras or something. But he took a chance on me and that scene became so famous, people in the entertainment business still remember me in it. It was used as an example of great directing in a class at UCLA film school.

Shirley and I went to the screening and afterward they had a big party at the Director's Guild building on Sunset. The casting director was sitting behind me in the theater and gave me a big compliment on my scene. Later, I ran into the editors and they said, "Art, we had one helluva time editing that scene."

I said, "Why?"

The editor said, "Because there was so much good stuff we didn't know what to cut out."

Then the assistant editor told me even more. She said, "Art, we had to cut out some stuff, because they didn't want you to steal the scene from Albert." This was my first feature film and I was flying five feet off the ground because everyone was coming over and complimenting me. It turned out to be kind of a cult film. That scene was really the beginning of my career.

After *Lost in America*, I started to get other parts, *The Young and the Restless*, for one. Unfortunately, if the agent I had at the time knew what the hell he was doing and had really promoted me when I was hot, I think I would be a lot further along in my career than I am. But it didn't happen; I just plugged away and have had several different agents since then.

I still got some great jobs, though. I was just getting out of bed one morning when the phone rang; the voice asked, "Is this Art Frankel from *Lost in America*?" I said yeah. He said, "How'd you like to have a part working with Jack Lemmon and Ted Danson?" He was the executive producer of a film called *Dad* with Jack Lemmon, Ted Danson, Olympia Dukakis, and Ethan Hawke.

I thought for a minute and then said, "I think I could handle that."

I played a DMV examiner. In the movie, Jack Lemmon's in his eighties and he wants to renew his license and his son, Ted Danson, is kind of tutoring him on the driver's test. I had to throw Ted Danson out of the car. Most of my time on the set I spent listening to Jack Lemmon tell his stories about the history of Hollywood, working with Marilyn Monroe — all the great things he'd experienced. He was a legend in his time, and one of the nicest guys I've ever met. It seems to me that the bigger the star, the nicer they are. I did a play called *Mass Appeal* once and Jack later starred in the movie. I told him, "I was so elated when I saw the movie that you made some of the same choices I did in the play."

And he said, "That just shows you, you got it." Just the nicest guy.

Since he was playing an eighty-seven-year-old man in *Dad*, his head was shaved. At the wrap party, Shirley went over and kissed him on his bald head. He really was the nicest guy you'd ever want to meet.

On the other hand, I worked on the film *Freaky Friday* a few years ago with Lindsay Lohan, Mark Harmon, and Jamie Lee Curtis. Lindsay's mother was there because Lindsay was only sixteen. Lindsay wouldn't even say hello to me when I passed her on the set. She was a real snob and I couldn't make out what was the matter. I talked to her mother quite a bit and told her I'd been a high school counselor and had worked with kids and said, "You know, you should really do something to keep Lindsay grounded; she seems like she might be going off in the wrong direction."

"No," her mother replied, "she's fine; there's nothing wrong with her." I said okay, and we all know how that story has played out. I honestly think that if people are decent and kind, and care about others, they're that way whether they're a big star or not and stardom doesn't spoil them. I think Lindsay was just like that and to this day, she still seems that way.

I'll never forget working with Tony Danza on *Who's the Boss*. His real-life son was about seventeen at the time and after I told him about being a high school counselor, we talked about college, that kind of stuff. When I went to say goodbye to him, I went to shake his hand, but he put his arms around me and kissed me. His co-star Judith Light also kissed me goodbye.

I played a priest on *Cagney and Lacey*. It was one of those rare instances where I went in for the audition and they cast me on the spot. I played opposite Sharon Gless as a priest in a confessional and while we were walking up to it she said, "Oh my God, I haven't been to confession in seventeen years."

I said, "Well, I haven't been to a confessional, either, but if you want to know what I did at my bar mitzvah, I'll tell you."

She broke up and said, "Oh my God, of all the people in L.A., we had to get a Jewish priest!" She was great to work with. She also loved what I did and kissed me goodbye, too.

I worked with Debra Messing and Thomas Haden-Church in *Ned and Stacey*, which was a fun show. My son came to see me shoot my episode. I had a bit part in *Death Wish 4*, with Charles Bronson. Whenever they stopped shooting or had lunch, he'd go off by himself; he didn't really talk to anybody. That's just who he was.

Sometimes you get a part and they shoot it, but they don't use it and you still get paid. Once I got a job on the movie *Evolution*. I got in make-up, and got my wardrobe, but when I came out of the trailer, the wind was just howling. One of the assistant directors told me, "Hey Art, we cancelled the shoot today because it's too windy. We'll probably pick it up again in January." Well, they never did pick it up. I got paid for the day and I'm still getting residuals for something I never did. Once I got a job over the phone and then they wrote the part out, but I got paid for that, too.

When I did *Freaky Friday*, I worked six days. The first day, the woman who was scheduled to play my wife in the wedding scene was two hours late, so we filmed it without her. The next day, she got lost and never showed up at all. They finally just gave me a background person (sometimes called an "extra") to play my wife. When they finally edited the movie, the missing wife caused too much of a problem so I was still in the film, but they cut out all my lines. I made something like $7000 for the six days — but a year or so later the movie came out, and one day I got a check in the mail for $43,000! I called up SAG and asked, "Is this a mistake?"

I was told, "No, it's your DVD residuals for *Freaky Friday*." All together on that film I made about $97,000 in DVD residuals and I didn't even audition for it; I got it from a demo tape.

A similar thing happened with the movie *The Ring*, starring Naomi Watts. I was in a scene that took place on an island in Puget Sound with a doctor, played by Jane Alexander. I played the part of an old crab fisherman, and I had to be there about seven in the morning for my scale rate of around $1000 a day. Well, I waited around through the morning, I ate lunch, I went down by the set and took a nap …. finally, at a quarter after six they shot the wide shot with me in it. When we got that, I had to wait longer because they still weren't finished with me. At 12:15 the next morning, they shot me over-the-shoulder. I ended up getting $3000 for saying one line to Jane Alexander while the camera was on the back of my head. Sometimes you're lucky, sometimes you're not — that's just the way the entertainment business is!

On *The Young and the Restless* I played a restaurant owner who borrowed money from a loan shark. In the scene I was trying to explain to the "shark" that I couldn't make the payment because my wife was in the hospital. His character said, "Well, we'll have to teach you what it means to have the proper protection." He had these two big thugs, and he said, "I'm gonna have to see what my favorite piranhas have to say." The thugs stuck my hands in this fish tank filled with killer piranhas and they chewed off my character's fingers! When it was finally on TV Shirley got so upset she started crying.

Acting is one of the most enjoyable things I've ever done and I can't imagine at my age that they pay me to do this. Financially, it's all worked out okay. I retired from SAG when I was sixty-two or sixty-three and as I mentioned, I get $1,000 a month from teacher's retirement, some odds and ends from other jobs I did over the years, about $300 a month in Social Security, and when I turned sixty-five, $176 a month from SAG. Fortunately, I earned enough from age fifty-five through sixty-five to get vested for life from SAG's health and retirement plans. But I kept on working, and found out that every year you make over $15,000 they take 3½ percent and add it to the next year's retirement. Pretty soon I got up to about $500 a month from SAG, and I thought that was great. Well, this year I'm up to $1464 a month in SAG retirement and next year it's going to up again to well over $1500. My Social Security has gone up from $300 a month to $1,064 because I've been contributing from the acting and the residuals. And then suddenly my teacher's retirement almost doubled to $2,300 and I'm still able to collect unemployment in between acting jobs. I can't complain about a thing now! When I retired I wondered how I was going to make it! Whoever heard of making more money after you retire than you did when you were working full-time?! When I left Fountain Valley High, I was at the top of the salary schedule which was $33,000 a year. I did one commercial for Aricept in 2006 and I made $55,000 on one commercial! I can't believe I'm this lucky and having this much fun at eighty-one years old!

I haven't been nominated for an Emmy or an Academy Award or anything, but all in all I've been in about fifteen feature films, a lot of TV, and gotten a ton of satisfaction out of it. Some people ask, "How come you didn't start acting younger in your life?"

I just say, "I had a real good career as a teacher and a counselor and I think I did a lot of good for a lot of people and left a lot of neat things behind. I don't regret what I did with my life; this is just another phase, going on to something else."

When I substitute I still tell the kids what I really believe: "never, ever retire; just keep changing careers." Whatever you do in life, you should be happy doing it because no matter how much money you make, it's not guaranteed to make you happy. You see it all the time, people who are greedy and have more money than they could ever use but they're just miserable. Some of them end up in jail because what they have they've stolen from others.

Chapter Twenty- Five

I can still remember that dark, horrible morning with the wind howling and the fire racing up toward our Arrowhead dream house. Luckily, Shirley and I got out of our neighborhood alive. We were able to make it down the hill to safety, but Rochelle got stuck in traffic up in Lake Arrowhead. We went out to Ontario to a new shopping center and realized that neither of us had eaten anything so we went to Applebee's. We were pretty upset and when we told the waitress why, our breakfast was comped. We called our daughter Nancy and gathered together all our animals and stuff and went to her house and watched the news.

Our neighbor Mike didn't leave. He drove over to nearby Twin Peaks where he has a brother and together they were stomping out embers. He called to tell us that he made it back to the top of our street and saw our house go down. Shirley called Rochelle on her cell and told her that the house was gone; Mike had watched it go.

The fact that our house had been destroyed was pretty traumatic. We had no idea what we were going to do, or how we were going to handle it. Eventually, Rochelle came down and joined us at Nancy's. Funny, the little things you remember. I called up Dish Network the next day to tell them to cancel my account because we didn't have a house anymore. I got transferred to some supervisor who got all official with me.

"If you cancel your account, you have to send back the Dish equipment."

I said, "I don't have any Dish equipment; it's kind of ruined."

He kept on and finally I said, *screw you*, and hung up on him. Someone called back and said, "If you don't cancel your account you don't have to send the equipment back right now; you can just leave it on hold for six months."

I said, "Okay, fine." People don't believe this, but Dish Network called me back for a whole year. One month it was resolved, the next month they'd call me to send the equipment back, then the next month everything was okay, and the next month we got some prepaid UPS boxes to ship the equipment back in. This went on until we were in the new house and they still sent us boxes to ship the equipment back. I was ready to take a piece of junk from the ashes and mail it back to them and say, "This is what's left of your equipment!"

The next day we called the insurance company that immediately sent us a $25,000 check for living expenses. Somehow things have fallen my way my whole life, and I don't know why.

Once I was driving across the railroad tracks in Davenport, Iowa and I heard a bell ringing, but I didn't see any gate come down so I drove over the tracks — and just as I cleared the tracks, a freight train screamed through right behind me.

Another time Shirley and I were in our BMW; Shirley was driving because I'd had a bilateral bunionectomy on both of my toes. All of a sudden this big four-door Mercury came barreling at us from the opposite direction — we were on the inside lane along the center divider. Shirley tried to get out of the way, but the Mercury hit her right behind the driver's seat on the center post. It bent the car and was a total loss. Shirley had all these curlers in her hair and the shock of the impact threw all her curlers into the back seat. We both walked away from it, thank God. I got out, grabbed my crutches (I needed them because of the surgery), while people watched us thinking, "Man, that was fast — the car wreck just happened; how did he already get crutches?" That was another disaster Shirley and I averted.

It's always been that way. I was on a B-25 with an engine on fire and I didn't have to jump; I decided to go into acting and make more money than I ever have ... well, my insurance coverage is exactly the same thing.

We were insured through AARP which uses Hartford Insurance, and in August of 2007, just two months before the fire, I decided to call them and ask them what my coverage was. The policy said the house was insured for $332,000 so I called and asked, "$332,000 wouldn't cover rebuilding the house if it ever goes. Do I have full replacement value?" They said yes, so I hung up and never thought about it again.

The sheriff and fire departments didn't allow us to come back up to Arrowhead for eight to ten days. We tried to come back earlier, but they had official vehicles blocking off all the streets. They were putting in new electrical poles and other telephone and utility lines and they didn't want people getting in the way.

As soon as they allowed us to come back, I called the insurance adjuster and met her by a Stater Brothers grocery store down the hill. She seemed nice, born in Malaysia, who immigrated to this country and became a citizen.

When we went up to look at the destruction and dig through the rubble, nobody could believe the intensity of the fire and the devastation it had caused. The insurance adjuster couldn't stop taking pictures of everything. The manager of the Home Depot in San Bernardino left each house little bouquets of flowers, shovels, face-masks, bottles of water, and screens so each household could sift through the rubble and ashes to see if they could find anything worth salvaging. It was such a nice feeling that someone cared! I really have to commend that manager; in fact, I met her later when I was down there shopping and told her how I felt about what they had done.

As we looked through the rubble, we wore special boots, gloves, and face masks. What we found just blew us away. We found all my stained glass windows, except the lead and glass had melted into blobs. The charred wreckage that was left of the old pot-bellied stove sat down at the bottom of our lot. In the concrete floor of the build-up I had installed a safe where I kept our important papers. The morning of the fire, I didn't open the safe and take the papers with me because I figured they would be safe buried down in the concrete. We uncovered it in the rubble to discover that the dial was gone … charred. Some husky kids we knew who worked for the Forest Service helped me crack the concrete with sledge hammers and take out the safe. It was impossible to open so I took it to a locksmith in Chino who had to cut it open. My passports had survived, my car registration and titles had survived, but my discharge from the service and my living trust were charred and melted together. Incredibly, the heat had transferred through the metal all the way to the inside. The devastation was complete. My home, everything I had left behind, was reduced to ash and charred ruins.

The insurance adjuster asked me if we were going to rebuild. My kids Jeff and Nancy didn't want us to rebuild in Arrowhead; they thought driving the crooked highway up the narrows was too dangerous for me, and as we were getting older we were closer to all the doctors down the hill. But I told the adjuster we liked living in Arrowhead and we were going to rebuild. She informed me that some people were using their insurance settlements to repay their mortgages.

I said, "How are they doing that?"

She said, "Speak to your builder."

So I spoke to my builder … and we don't have a mortgage anymore!

Chapter Twenty-Six

We were still living in Huntington Beach when I did *Lost in America* and we'd sworn to God that we'd never move again, but the condo we were living in looked out on a fence and the parking lot of the Huntington Beach High School. The front window in the living room looked at the wall of the garage, and there were no windows on either side because our condo was a middle unit; we really felt closed in. We'd come to enjoy Arrowhead during our trips up for the acting seminars, so we drove up, checked in with a real estate agent and bought a lot in 1995 for $33,000. We rented our Huntington Beach condo to a woman with an option to buy, but she had bad credit and couldn't come up with financing and so she had to move out. We had an agreement with her where we kept all our furniture stored in the garage. We had a kitty door in there because we left two of our cats behind. What also took up residence in the garage was a family of skunks! When we finally went to move our stuff out, we had to get rid of skunks! We finally sold the condo in January of 1998 for around $235,000 and got the cash out of it, although we had also gotten a construction loan from a bank in Redlands. Our mortgage on the new house was around $145,000 with mortgage payments around $1000 a month.

When we first looked at our lot on Marin Lane, a lot of trees were on it so it was kind of hard to tell what kind of view we would have. I stood on a big rock and looked out and said, "Well, maybe the first floor would be around here with that view, and up around the street level we could have the main floor with that ..." We really didn't want a lot without a view and we couldn't afford a place down by the lake.

When we decided to move, we originally were planning to go to Ojai, a quiet community in the hills above Ventura, California, not too far from the beach. Why Ojai? Well, after I sold the "Sarah Ann," I bought a twenty-eight-foot Southern Cross from Bristol, Rhode Island that I named, "L' Chaim," which in Hebrew means "to life." During Easter vacation of 1982, Jeff and I were sailing her off the Channel Islands and a real heavy wind came up, so we decided to go into the harbor at Ventura. We started up the engine, and planned on pulling the sails down and motor in, when all of a sudden the prop shaft broke. Oh shit! Whoever installed the engine didn't line up the prop shaft properly. If it isn't lined up, it will wobble, and will finally work itself until it breaks.

We didn't have a prop shaft, and a little water was running into the engine room. We had to put up the sails, with the wind blowing like hell, but somehow we managed to limp back into Channel Islands Harbor, which is quite a distance north of Long Beach Harbor. We called Shirley to tell her where we were and what had happened, then we called Rhode Island to order a new prop shaft, but we had to wait for it to come all that way. We had the boat hauled out and put into dry dock and then proceeded to live on the boat in the shipyard. We had a little barbecue we put on the ground and used the restrooms in the shipyard. Just our luck, that Easter vacation Rhode Island had a big snowstorm, which delayed delivery of the prop shaft even further. Because of the stress and the tension and the sun, I had a cold sore develop on the right side of my nose that went down my upper lip and along my lower lip. There I was with this humongous cold sore that had to be two inches long and I was living in the shipyard! Eventually the prop shaft arrived at my address in Huntington Beach and Shirley drove it up to us in Oxnard. On the way up, she went through Ventura, saw the scenery in nearby Ojai, and just loved it.

After installing the prop shaft, we drove up to Ojai and found a gated community that was being built. We bought a beautiful lot, about two-and-a-half acres that had live oak trees on it. We didn't have the money for the down, so we borrowed $30,000 against our duplex in Huntington Beach. As we started thinking about what kind of house we were going to build, I got all jazzed up about geodesic domes. This has been the story of my life, always into new things, something that no one else ever has. The homeowner's association didn't like the idea of the geodesic dome one bit. We went back and forth — they said they wouldn't allow it, and someone made some remarks about Judaism. The attorney we'd hired said, "You should take them to court for discrimination; that's anti-Semitism!"

We never did. The whole thing went down the tubes and we lost the lot. Shirley got a second job to help pay off the $30,000 loan. We finally sold our duplex on 18th Street and that's when we turned our attention to Lake Arrowhead. Ojai was a financial disaster, but looking back, Arrowhead turned out to be a much better choice, climate-wise and for proximity to my family and Los Angeles.

I moved up in Labor Day of 1996 and rented a house for myself and our two grandsons who were living with me at the time. Shirley was still working down in Mission Viejo so she came up on weekends and lived with our daughter Cindy in Huntington Beach. She worked until December 31, 1997 and then moved up permanently. I, of course, was still commuting back and forth between Arrowhead and Hollywood for auditions and acting jobs.

After checking around, we hired a builder named Ron Rawls. I wanted to live up there while we were building because I wanted to be on the construction site every day. I was originally going to build the house myself and sub out all the jobs, like a homeowner/builder, but I started to look at the things I had to do, and the permits I had to get, and the challenge of building in the side of a mountain, and the people I'd have to hire not knowing the subcontractors and who would do this and who would do that … I finally just hired a builder. I got a recommendation from the real estate agent who'd sold me the lot. I checked him out and he seemed to be very reliable; he was in his sixties and he'd been doing construction since he was twenty-one, and then he became a contractor. He'd been working up in Arrowhead for over twenty years.

I'm the kind of guy who's there every day bugging the hell out of anyone doing anything. At one point, Shirley said to Ron, "Are you sure you want to build a house with my husband?" We designed the house and decided how to build it. The altitude is about 5400 feet on Marin Lane, with a lot of cedars, oaks, and pine we had to cut down. I decided that I wanted to have a pot-bellied stove, so we saved all the wood, cut it up into firewood, and stored it underneath the house. I later found out that cedar or pine can't be burned in a stove because it has a lot of sap and it clogs up the chimney. We had a chimneysweep come and clean things out, because the spark arrestor got completely clogged up. I haven't burned pine or cedar since.

We decided to have four bedrooms. The master bedroom was over the garage, with the kitchen, dining room, living room and half-bath and laundry room on the main floor, which was almost street level. We had a master bath and another full bath down on the bottom level along with three bedrooms. We had two forty-gallon hot water heaters down behind a door in the build-up, an extra one for the whirlpool tub. We broke ground in January of 1997. All the forms were there and they were going to pour the concrete on a Monday in the middle of January. Ron called up that Saturday and said if I wanted to see it poured I'd better come over right away because a big storm was coming. The crew poured sixty yards of concrete, and sure enough, Sunday night the storm came and covered everything in snow. I don't know how many feet it was, but you couldn't see a thing, it was so thick. The street out front had only one lane plowed through it. It took two weeks before all the snow melted and all the water ran out from underneath so they could work.

As I mentioned, my two grandsons Jacob and Brent were living with me during this period of time. My daughter Rochelle and her first husband John, with whom she had the two boys, lived with us for a while because of some financial difficulties. Finally she divorced him and married Tim the Marine sergeant. He lived with us for a while and is the father of our granddaughter Adama. Not long after, they got divorced. Tim was stationed over at 29 Palms and kept Adama over there. The two boys were going to school at J.D. Smith Jr. High for a while and it was a real confusing situation. Tim would come and stay sometimes on the weekends, but they were divorced. By the time we moved to Beach Walk, Rochelle had married Robert.

By the time we moved in 1996, Tim had adopted the boys and tried to care for them alone, but it didn't work out and they ended up in the social service system. Shirley felt really bad for them and so we decided to take them in.

Jacob was the older one and Brent was younger by two years; at the time they were both in high school. Unfortunately, both of them had their struggles in school. I eventually moved Jacob over to continuation school because he wasn't making it in the regular high school. The thing was, Jacob was a great golfer. He joined the golf team at Rim of the World High School, and he played and practiced at the Arrowhead Country Club. At eighteen-years-old, before he got any instruction from anybody, he could look at golfers and tell them exactly what was wrong with their swing and how to improve it. I used to take him down to the golf course and he was able to play there because he'd give the members tips. When I'd pick him up people would say, "Thanks so much for letting me play with your grandson. He improved my game enormously."

Because of this, I decided to send him to a golf college in Temecula. It's a two-year AA degree program. But the program began in January and I had to get him graduated from high school first. I stayed up until four in the morning with him reading Anne Frank's diary, making book reports, etc. so he could graduate the next day. Finally we got all the credits in and he graduated and off he went to golf college. He wasn't too keen on the idea, and for some reason he thought we were just trying to get rid of him. I said, "Jake, this is an ideal chance for you to go learn golf and get your PGA card so you can earn fifty bucks an hour teaching golf. You're a natural at it; once you get your PGA card you can make some good money." Well he went, but I had to talk him into finishing. He got his AA degree, but to this day still doesn't have his PGA card. He's thirty-years-old, and moved to Ft. Lauderdale, where he works for a blood bank. He recruits people to donate blood and he's very successful at it.

Brent is 6 foot 4 and weighs 280. When he lived with us, he was a klutz, but really a sweet kid! He wanted a snake, so we got him a snake. He had to have a heater for the snake, which he put down on the carpet. He didn't check to see if it was plugged in and it burned a hole right through. He just turned twenty-eight. He's worked at different jobs but he's bi-polar and has other issues. He didn't graduate from high school, but I took him to Riverside and helped him get his GED. He's got a beautiful little baby girl, but he can't seem to hold a job; he's just not that confident. His girlfriend is working and doing very well, so he stays home and plays on the computer, babysits, and takes care of his daughter while she supports the family. That's how those boys wound up: one's taking care of his little girl and not in jail and the other's working and making a living, so what can I say?

I would try to tell them about my value system, about how before you can be successful in life you have to have everyday skills: how to use a checkbook, how to live in a house, do your own laundry, mundane things that everyone has to do. They would never listen to my advice. They're finding out now, years later, that you have to have those little skills so you can survive on a daily basis. It was tough.

I said to Jacob just the other day, "Grandma and I tried to raise you, teach you some values, teach you things and we have no clue whether or not you got anything."

Jacob replied, "You're not my mom and dad. You may not think so, but I got all my political values from you. I know my father wasn't Jewish, but everything about your values, about Judaism, about politics, everything I got from you. You taught me a lot."

That meant a lot to me.

We love living here, we love the scenery, we love the climate; the big problem is driving into town. I have to drive between eighty-five and one hundred miles each way going up and down the mountain and then when I have commercials I have a call-back, so I have to go in a second time. Many times I end up driving four hundred miles and I still don't get the part. That's the only bad part of the acting profession. The acting itself, I love — being in front of a camera, being on set. To me, it's just a blast that they pay me to do silly stuff in front of a camera.

Chapter Twenty-Seven

Marry someone you truly love.

Shirley and I celebrated our sixtieth wedding anniversary in January of 2010. On our fiftieth anniversary, our daughter Nancy, who always does everything for everybody, arranged a surprise party at Marie Callender's down in Chino. She told us, "Dress up because we're going to take you out to dinner at a really fancy place." Somehow she'd gotten our address book. All our neighbors in the mountains were there, and my sister flew in from North Carolina. My daughter-in-law Sandy met her back East, paid for her flight, and accompanied her back to California specifically to surprise us. The whole time we had no clue about any of this. We arrived at Marie Callender's, thinking we were going to a nice dinner, and all of a sudden everyone yelled, "Surprise!!" Nancy had gotten a minister, and a chuppah like you have at a Jewish wedding. We had a great party and renewed our vows. Our daughter even had gotten us a wedding cake.

When Shirley and I decided to get married the first time around, I don't even know if I officially asked her or not. I don't remember getting down on my knees and asking her to marry me — I'd been going with her for two years. I was about to finish my sophomore year and go back to Connecticut to work at the resort for the summer, but by then, I realized if I had to leave Shirley behind I just couldn't do that. I'd met the person I wanted to spend the rest of my life with. We never had any training or experience in running a house or finances or anything like that. When we got married, Shirley didn't even know how to cook. But the reason I married her was that I just did not want to leave her. I wanted to be with her and that was it.

Shirley never said no to me, whether it was sexually or anything else. She was a virgin when we got married. She learned to really enjoy making love and appreciate the intimacy to the point where to this day, she still tries to please me. Our moments in the bedroom have helped us over many rough patches in our marriage. Recently, Shirley was laughing on the phone while talking to one of our daughters and when she hung up I asked what was so funny. Shirley and our daughters are very close; they even discuss sex. Shirley still allows me to indulge in sexual activity once a week on Sunday morning, which works out okay because my health plan only allows me one Viagra per week. Shirley was laughing so hard on the phone because it turns out that she and I are more active than some of our kids and their friends! I asked my urologist if it was unusual for men in their eighties to still be sexually active and he said it wasn't, so there! Don't ever pass up an opportunity to make love to your wife.

Shirley always tried to do everything she could to please me even though I wasn't the greatest husband at first. When I went back to Drake I would want to hang out with the guys; there were some nights when I was out in the snow with my car and chains, helping people dig out and she didn't know where the hell I was. I guess I wasn't completely sensitive to her feelings. She was an only child and I was her only support. But there was something about her — she was so nice to me and so good — that I finally felt guilty about being such a jerk. I came around and have changed a helluva lot since I was a young man. When I look back now, I didn't help out with the kids like I should have, I didn't do housework or dishes. I took care of all the outside and mechanical stuff, fixing things and changing the oil on the cars. If we had to do it all over, I would help her out more than I did.

She always went along with my crazy ideas. Moving all over the country, teaching here, teaching there … no matter what I suggested she'd say, "Oh no, not again."

When I said, "let's forget everybody, all the family, your mother, my parents, and move out to Henderson," she went along with it. When we moved around and bought different houses and had to borrow money here and there she went along with me. When we had tenants, people would move in and out and we had to paint the apartments and fix things up ourselves, she wasn't too jazzed about that, I can tell you! But she went along with it.

I went to Europe three summers in a row with high school kids on tours and she was alone with the kids at home; she wasn't too happy, but she let me go. One summer I went around the U.S. for six weeks with high school kids; I was gone and she made it possible for me to go. Another summer I was up in the mountains with Carl Stal backpacking, and our son Jeff, who was only about sixteen or seventeen, went down to Ensenada. He was walking along with a sealed bottle of booze sticking out of his pocket and got arrested for stopping to help an American who had passed out on the hood of a car. As Jeff gave up on him and walked away, the police chased him down when they went to arrest the passed-out gentleman. Shirley had to go down there with my cousin Marty and bail him out of jail. But through it all, Shirley never complained. She's just an amazing lady, always going along with all my crazy ideas. That's the lady I married and stayed with because she's been so nice and perfect for me.

She is truly my lover and best friend. She worked most of our marriage, came home and cooked dinner, cleaned the house, baked cakes and cookies for the family even though she is gluten-intolerant and can't eat them. On weekends, she did all the shopping, kept on top of all the birthday and greeting cards, and took care of me. With all my trips and all our moves around the country, she never whined. In fact, she encouraged me. When I said we should sell our house and buy the three triplexes, no problem. When I invested in two different land deals, she said okay. When I sold the triplexes and built a boat, I don't remember any complaints. Today those triplexes are worth 2.5 million dollars. I tell her that and she just smiles. She's scared to death of the ocean, but she got on a boat and sailed to Hawaii and brought the book *Jaws* to read.

When we moved to the mountains and built our first house, she said, "You know what would look good in those semi-circle windows over the sliding glass doors?"

I said, "No, what?"

She said, "Stained-glass windows."

I said, "They're very expensive." I had priced them in 1997, and they were $2500 a window.

She said, "Why don't you do them? They have a class at this stained-glass store." At first I said no, but in the end I gave in. I made three six-foot windows, a lamp for my daughter Nancy, two windows for my daughter Cindy, and several other windows for friends and neighbors. Shirley has this blind faith in me that I can do anything I put my mind to. Since we moved to the mountains and semi-retired, I have a great deal of time to read. She reads the *L.A. Times* book review every Sunday and picks out books she thinks I would like. I tell her, "Don't buy me any books." She does anyway. In fact, her choices are always pretty good.

She's bought all my clothes to make sure I'm in style and dressed properly to this day. She's always been a great mother. All the kids love her and show it. How many families do you know where their daughters want to go away for the weekend with their mother? She's a kind, caring, loving, thoughtful person. How does anyone find a wife like this? I don't know; I was most fortunate. The old cliché "behind every good man is a great woman" happens to be true in my case.

One thing that's wrong with her, even though she doesn't think so, is that she always puts herself down. I love Shirley more than I have the words to express. She has a great sense of humor, and she knows how to laugh at herself. My son Jeff loves to tease her and make her laugh. She's the neatest lady you'd ever want to meet. I can't imagine having a better wife than the one I've had.

And the most amazing thing is that Shirley and I ever met at all. Because there is one thing I haven't told you about our childhood yet. And it is a story that you won't believe …

Chapter Twenty-Eight

Shirley's parents couldn't have children, and were in their early forties when they adopted Shirley. They were Jews from Lithuania who had settled in Des Moines and were looking for a Jewish baby. They talked to their rabbi who told them he knew of an adoption agency. He had no idea that he was putting them in touch with a villainous, corrupt organization run by a woman apparently devoid of morals, conscience, or even simple human decency. Her name was Georgia Tann and her agency was called the Tennessee Children's Home Society. Posing as a legitimate adoption agency, Georgia Tann made a fortune running a black market selling babies that her operatives had stolen from playgrounds, hospitals, and city streets. Like hundreds of other children, Shirley has no idea who her biological parents are, whether or not she has any biological siblings — or even what her real name is. And she will never know. The *Los Angeles Times* featured a story on Shirley a few years ago and she spoke for all the babies whom Georgia Tann stole from their homes when she said, "I have no history."

Georgia Tann, a lesbian who adopted a daughter of her own, was a criminal who caused an enormous amount of heartbreak. Can you imagine being a parent of a child, looking away for a moment, and then looking back to find him or her gone — and never seen again? Thanks to Georgia Tann, thousands of families experienced this nightmare and Shirley and her biological parents was one of them. Georgia Tann would steal babies from all over Memphis, falsify every bit of their records, new birth certificates, create relatives who didn't exist — and then put the kids up for adoption ... for a handsome fee.

Most of the people she stole babies from were poor, and didn't have money for attorneys. If they did report the kidnapping, the police wouldn't do anything, because Georgia was buddy-buddy with the mayor and the authorities, and had them all on the payroll. Tann's own father was a judge somewhere in Mississippi. There were cases where wealthy people needed a baby — perhaps their daughter's baby was born stillborn — and Georgia Tann would have a new baby right there the next day without the mother ever knowing that her baby was stillborn and that the baby she was holding wasn't really her child. That's how efficient she was at stealing kids.

Not only did she destroy homes, but she treated the kids in her care horribly. She was very negligent and her orphanage had the highest death rate in the area, losing nearly forty kids in just one year. There were multiple cases of her and her employees molesting kids. Shirley was very lucky that she survived and came out as good as she did. We're guessing that she didn't have proper infant nutrition or prenatal care because when she was in her twenties, she started to lose her teeth.

The Tennessee Children's Home Society was recommended to Shirley's adoptive parents because Georgia Tann had a Jewish attorney who was in contact with about 200 rabbis across the United States. If someone wanted a Jewish baby, Tann would just change the names on the records to make it look like a baby was Jewish. In Shirley's case, they took the records of a Hazel Beale. Hazel had her baby sometime in the fall of 1931, so Georgia Tann gave Shirley a birthday of Sept 9, 1931, and then changed all the records in the hospital. She said that Shirley's father's name was William Cohen and her mother was Hazel Beale (all made up!) Her falsified story was that they were high school kids, unwed parents — the records even had made-up relatives who didn't exist. She had doctors and nurses at the hospital working for her, and a Memphis judge in her pocket; she had everybody.

We have no clue about Shirley's real parents or where she came from; we don't even know her real birthday. When I was selling cars for Saturn I went through the Spring Hill Auto Plant in Tennessee, and I contacted an attorney in nearby Nashville. I paid the attorney $500 to get the records. I had to go through an attorney because the records were legally closed in Tennessee until the year 2000, which was several years later. I met the attorney in a hotel lobby.

She handed them to me and said, "These are the strangest records I've ever seen."

I said, "Why?"

She said, "Look through them and find out."

I did, and it blew my mind because it was all just stuff that didn't exist.

How Shirley came into Georgia Tann's hands, we will never know. According to the records, I saw that when Shirley's adopted mother got her, Shirley was supposed to be about six months old. But that's based on the birthday Georgia Tann gave her, so we don't know for sure. Georgia Tann tended to make the birthdays later so the kids looked more mature and older than they really were. The only way that Shirley can find out what group of people she comes from is to get a DNA test, which we are currently in the process of doing. At least then she will know her overall ancestry, although finding any possible biological family members will always be a mystery. We did do a DNA search through the National Geographic program, but the best we could find out is that Shirley's ancestors were from western Europe. Without knowing her real last name, it is impossible to find more specific information. * *See Appendix.*

Chapter Twenty-Nine

I've read that after a fire or other disaster where everything is lost, a person often falls into a state of depression. That didn't happen to me or Shirley or Rochelle. What was depressing was the house that Shirley and Rochelle rented for us to live in while we were rebuilding. They were afraid they wouldn't find anything, because the fire had created a situation where a lot people were looking for places to rent. They panicked and rented a house that was a disaster in and of itself. The house was old and the heating system was old and totally inadequate. Some heating ducts ended inside cabinets or in closets and the previous owners just left them there. Some rooms were too hot, others too cold. In the summer, the whole house was like an oven. There was a steep driveway that turned into the garage; it was hell digging out when it snowed. The gas and electric bills in November and December were about $400 a month. I called the landlord and told him we were thinking of moving because of all the inconvenience. He offered to clear the driveway when it snowed and pay the utilities.

There were too many other repairs to mention, but trust me, everything needed fixing. The thing nobody could fix was the configuration of the house. After carefully maneuvering our car up the steep driveway and around the corner into the garage, we locked the garage and had to walk outside up a steep stairway to the front door. Once inside, we had to climb to the main floor on another steep, narrow stairway that didn't have a banister on one side, from which we could easily fall. They had to fix that. We were thinking of moving, but it seemed like more trouble than it was worth. I was busy planning and building the house with the builder every day anyway and the girls were busy shopping.

My goal was to get back into the new house as soon as possible. The fire happened on October 22, 2007 and we moved back in to our new house on October 13, 2008. The new house took a little longer to rebuild than our original house because the new house was a lot more elaborate. I think in the end we didn't get depressed because we simply had no time.

Chapter Thirty

There is no greater treasure than your family.
Don't ever take them for granted.

I've always wondered what kind of father I was. As I mentioned, my wife and I didn't have a clue about raising children and they don't come with a set of instructions. When they're babies it's easy to follow your pediatrician's advice about feeding and other physical needs. But then your children begin to assert themselves, they become little people, and you can't be in complete control. As they grow and mature, you have to grow and mature with them. You have to know how much freedom to give them, how much authority to let go, and at what point to do it. It is a difficult process, which is why many parents try to keep the same level of control from early childhood, even when their kids are rebellious teenagers. It doesn't work.

Another big issue is that all children are not the same. One set of rules and regulations can not be applied equally to all children. They all have different abilities and needs. As parents, we have to teach them the standards that society expects them to live by. The moral standards that we expect in their behavior, we can set as an example.

While growing up I heard the statement from parents to, "do as I say, not as I do." It doesn't work. Our children will follow what we do. Some kids will almost always do the right thing at school and at home and will never be a problem; if they make a mistake we just have to remind them what is proper. When my daughter Nancy was growing up, she always did the best whether at home or at school. If she did something wrong, which wasn't very often, all I had to say was that I was disappointed and she would straighten up. My son, on the other hand, was a straight-A student through eighth grade and then he discovered girls and pot and beer. We were constantly at odds, fighting about grades and behavior. I was very concerned and one day I was taking a walk by myself, trying to analyze what was happening. I wasn't happy with our relationship and I remembered something I'd read in a book. I think the name of the book was *Between Parent and Teenager*. The main theme was "avoid conflict." I thought that was good advice, so the next report card he brought home for me to sign, I looked it over, picked out all the good acceptable grades, congratulated him and ignored the unacceptable ones. I signed it and handed it back to him. He knew what I was doing and he smiled. He never became a straight-A student again, but we didn't fight about report cards anymore. We avoided conflict. He didn't do all the things that I suggested he do with his life, but he's an adult and he turned out to be my best friend (next to my wife).

Every family member must take responsibility for doing what they are supposed to do to make the family function properly. Sign a contract with each child if that's what it takes. When they break the contract, they must pay the consequences. No arguments, no conflicts. I don't claim to be the best parent, but I take pride in the fact that all five of our children are our best friends and are constantly in touch. The most important thing is to make sure your children know you love them. Parents often bring up their kids just the way they were brought up because they are scripted to automatically repeat their parents' actions, even though they hated what they did. My father used a lot of corporal punishment on me and I thought that was wrong. It took me a long time to change my script. Every once in a while I'd fall back into it and I had to discipline myself to keep myself from doing what I knew was wrong. The biggest problem with young parents is that they don't know how to change the messages that their parents imprinted into them. Parents will repeat this unless they change their scripting.

As a family we've had more great times together than I can possibly mention. My daughter Debbie married her high school sweetheart in the backyard of our duplex on 18th Street. We were having margaritas and champagne, and of course, somebody had to bring out some pot. They talked Shirley and me into trying pot. Well, after drinking, marijuana doesn't go very well. Shirley tried it and she instantly retired to the bedroom; the room was spinning, her mouth turned into cotton, and she was out of it! I don't know if it affected me that much, but I didn't like it at all. Another time, not long after the wedding, one of my daughters' boyfriends brought some hash to our house. We put it under a glass and smoked it through a straw. I don't know what they saw in that stuff, but I'd rather have a good martini or gin and tonic.

My son Jeff and I did a lot of backpacking. Once we went to King's Canyon in Sequoia National Park and my daughter Debbie and her friend Marsha came along. We camped at a lake at 10,000 feet elevation; I think it was called Hidden Lake. I wasn't much of a fisherman, but I brought a collapsible rod and a Red Devil spinner. The lake was loaded with German brown trout. It seemed that they would bite at almost anything we threw out any time. We figured out how many trout we needed for each meal and we caught them. It was like shopping in a supermarket! We cleaned the fish and stored them in a nearby snow bank until meal time. We went swimming in that freezing lake and slid down a snow bank that was still there even though it was summer. Once when Jeff and I were walking on a trail, a ferocious-looking animal came running right by us, the size of a large dog. When we described it to a ranger, he said it was a wolverine and it was very rare sight. I guess we were lucky!

My daughter Debbie is a dear sweet lady and a lot like her mother, very devoted to the man she is with. The man she married in our backyard decided he was gay about a year later. They got divorced, but Debbie never stopped caring about him. He became a nurse and was in that profession until he contracted the HIV virus and died of AIDS, still in his twenties. Very sad. She married Paul after that, who was abusive and not a very nice or caring person. She divorced Paul after seven years and lives with Leonard in Chino. They're still not married; maybe she's gun-shy after her second marriage. She's been with Leonard for fifteen years or so and has an engagement ring. They have a big backyard and Debbie loves to grow all kinds of vegetables which she shares with the whole family. She is almost a year older than Rochelle and the two of them are the best of friends. They visit each other frequently and have a great deal of fun together.

Cindy is the baby, twelve years younger than my son Jeff and five years younger than Rochelle. She became the special little girl. Nancy kind of took her under her wing and they have a special bond. Cindy married Gordon and after living several years in Huntington Beach, they moved to Grass Valley, California. They live on a five-and-a-half acre lot on a gravel road almost two miles from a paved street. All sorts of wild animals wander past their property: deer, wild turkeys, bobcats, and even some bear. In fact, a bear killed one of their goats. Frontier living! The rest of the family was upset when she left because it's five hundred or so miles away and we don't see her family as much as we like. When she comes to visit, everyone wants her to stay at their house. She is a great deal of fun and a party animal.

In the old days, fathers weren't let into the delivery rooms, but when Rochelle was born the doctor said it was okay for me to come in and I actually saw her being born. When the doctor took her out and put her on a table in the delivery room, she was jumping around like a banshee — and she hasn't stopped since! We found out later, after she had a lot trouble in school, that she's bipolar and suffers from obsessive-compulsive disorder. I had to spend a lot of time with her just getting her through high school. She lives with us now full-time; we take care of her and she takes care of us. Unfortunately, OCD never goes away.

Chapter Thirty-One

*Always make time for family vacations, your
kids (and you) will never forget them.*

In 1964, I embarked on an 11,000 mile trip around the United States with high school students on a Greyhound bus. In 1972, I took my wife and three daughters on the same trip. Being a history teacher, I thought it was a great way to see the beauty of this country and visit historical places that gave our country its great legacy. Besides, I had a captive audience! The first night we camped near Flagstaff, Arizona. We visited the Painted Desert, the Petrified Forest, and then headed off to White Sands, New Mexico and the Carlsbad Caverns. There's no way I can describe these places in a book; you just have to see them in person. There's not much to see in west Texas; it's a pretty dry desert. The next stop was the Alamo, in San Antonio, a special place in the hearts of all Texans. Houston was next. Our goal was not to see the city, but to get our new BMW Bavaria serviced. I bought it in January of '72, a 3-liter four-door sedan. We decided to camp about half the time, and stay in motels the other half. With all the luggage we had, we brought along a pop-up tent.

There's so much to see in New Orleans, we saw what we could, but only got a quick sketch of the city: the French Quarter and the canal tours, the unique cemeteries above ground, Jackson Square, and so much history. It was part of the Louisiana Purchase and is one of the most important shipping ports then and to this day. We drove through Biloxi, Mississippi on our way to St. Augustine, Florida. In Biloxi, where I'd taken my army basic training at Keesler Field, we saw the home of Jefferson Davis, the president of the Confederacy.

St. Augustine, Florida is rich in history, being America's oldest city built in 1565. They also have beautiful white sand beaches that we enjoyed. We were on a schedule because we had to cover 11,000 miles in six weeks, so we didn't have time to see everything.

Along the South Carolina coast was Fort Sumter, an important historical site because the Civil War started there, another important milepost in our history. In Williamsburg, Virginia, we jumped back in time to colonial America; there's no place in the U.S. quite like it. It was exactly like it was before the Revolutionary War. In the area where tourists visit, no automobiles are allowed, only horses and carriages. The architecture and all the people are dressed in the manner of that period of history. It should be a required stop for all Americans. The House of Burgesses, the inns, the taverns, the gunsmiths, the cobblers, the fife and drum corps — all these places are authentic and indescribable. John Smith and Pocahontas are honored there and the girls had their pictures taken in the stocks, which were used for minor infractions instead of jail. By the way, the cobblers made shoes that were interchangeable, right and left. I didn't know that before; did you?

Appomattox Courthouse, where Lee and Grant signed the documents to end the Civil War, was one of our stops. I was also impressed with Monticello, Thomas Jefferson's home. He was an architect and designed the entire house and estate. He was an inventor, a writer, a statesman; I guess you might call him a Renaissance man. He even wrote his own version of the New Testament, eliminating all the miracles. I have a replica of his rain gauge on my deck.

Arlington National Cemetery and Washington, D.C. were next. We visited all the government buildings and monuments and museums, the White House, and many other famous buildings on the Washington Mall. We stopped at Mount Vernon, George Washington's home. We checked out the Gettysburg battlefield, considered the turning point of the Civil War.

Then it was on to Philadelphia where we toured Independence Hall, the Liberty Bell, and Ben Franklin's grave. We also visited with Shirley's aunt and her family.

"New York, New York — a wonderful town, the Bronx is up and the Bowery's down, people ride in a hole in the ground." Sound familiar? I was born in the Bronx, but grew up in Connecticut so I can't tell you about living there. I visited a great deal when I lived in Connecticut. I saw the 1939 World's Fair and my 1945 high school graduation class trip was spent there. Shirley and I saw Broadway shows several times there. There's no other city like it in the United States and it is rightfully considered to be one of the foremost cities in the world.

The World Trade Center wasn't finished then; the two top floors were just being completed. Of course, now it's gone. My sister and her family lived in Brooklyn then and my cousin Gertrude lived in lower Manhattan. We visited with them, and Gertrude being the consummate New Yorker, helped us with sightseeing. Of course we saw the typical sights like the Chrysler Building, the Empire State Building, and a circle boat tour around Manhattan Island. We also had to ride the subway.

Connecticut, my old stomping grounds, was next. We visited some relatives I grew up with, my cousins, the Klars, my uncle Herman, and my aunt Frieda. Before we left we visited the Mystic Seaport Marine Museum.

Next we stopped in Newport, Rhode Island to visit the Touro Synagogue, the first Jewish house of worship built in America, founded in 1658. Roger Williams established complete religious freedom in the colony of Rhode Island, and many Jews moved there for that reason. Touro Synagogue still has a functioning congregation and is an official National Historical Site.

From there we went to the famous Plymouth, Massachusetts, where the Pilgrims landed. Cape Cod was next on our agenda, for more sailing history with a great display of the women's figurines that were mounted on the bowsprits of the sailing vessels. Cape Cod village is quaint and picturesque with its own building and all the lobster café restaurants.

Boston is the city where much of our history began and being a history teacher at the time, there was a great deal of discussion about what we were seeing. I can't leave Boston without mentioning the USS Constitution called "Old Ironsides." It's the oldest commissioned warship in the world that is still afloat. I have a replica of it on my mantlepiece. It was launched in 1779, became famous in the War of 1812, defeating the British HMS De Guerre. While in Boston we visited Lexington and Concord. We drove north from Boston through Portsmouth, New Hampshire. We stopped along the Kennebec River in Maine which was jammed with logs floating to the sawmill.

We journeyed into Quebec and Montreal, sightseeing along the way. We stayed at Niagara Falls overnight and then crossed back into the U.S. into Michigan. When I was in Dearborn, Michigan in 1964, I saw the first Ford Mustang come off the assembly line. As you know, it later became a classic. Greenfield Village has some interesting sights, which we visited on the way to Des Moines. We stopped at the Kellogg plant. In Des Moines we visited with some of Shirley's relatives and took a picture in front of the synagogue where we got married. Shirley also wanted to visit her favorite cousin Kate, who had played a key role in Shirley's life when she was growing up. From there we headed to the national parks in the West.

The south part of South Dakota is pretty flat and desolate. I'll never forget our campground at Mount Rushmore. It was terraced into the side of a steep hill. We set up the camp and we were asleep when a real violent thunderstorm approached. I don't remember the exact time, maybe one or two in the morning; we all got up, packed up as quickly as possible. We were worried about getting washed down the hill. It started to rain before we packed up the tent, so it got soaked. We drove to the nearest motel, and unpacked the tent to dry it out. What a night! It was still cloudy and foggy the next day, so everyone stayed in the car. I was determined to get a picture of Mount Rushmore. I got out and waited. It partially cleared for a brief moment and I got picture through the fog; not very clear, but still a picture.

We left the Black Hills of South Dakota for Yellowstone National Park. We viewed Old Faithful, all the other boiling and steaming pools, and saw so much wildlife like deer and bears. The next scenic park was the Grand Tetons. I understand the French named this park and it means "Big Tits." Leave it to the French! We went swimming in the lake, and horseback riding in the mountains. Bryce and Zion National Parks were the last parks we visited. They're not far from each other, but completely different. Bryce with its bright red sandstone, and narrow canyons — Zion with massive rock domes where some places have symmetrical designs on the face of the cliffs.

We stopped in Las Vegas, camped overnight, and headed home the next day. Being together for weeks, we had our confrontations and hassles. In Arizona one of the girls left a box of crayons on the back seat under the window and it melted. I lost it! My new car! I accidentally stabbed a pen through the headliner, and of course, the girls had their tiffs also. This trip was not only important for its educational value, but it was six weeks of a family activity. It brought us much closer together. It was over thirty-one years ago and I remember it vividly and so do my girls. You may have heard this before, but children will remember and cherish the time you spent with them much more than the presents you bought for them.

Learning to relate well to kids can be difficult at times, but there are definitely some "don'ts" I've learned over the past eighty years, as a parent, a teacher, and counselor.

Parents shouldn't live vicariously through their children, like the dad who forces his son into sports because Dad didn't make it into professional sports. Or the mother who pushes her little girl into "beauty pageants" and says it was all her little girl's idea. Give me a break. Spend enough time with your children to know who they really are, learn what their interests are, and help them pursue <u>their</u> dreams, not yours. Making sure they get into medicine or law or sports because you think that's the best profession doesn't mean anything if they really want to be a dancer, an actor, or an artist. Down the road they will dislike you intensely for pushing them into something they don't enjoy doing.

And even if you really think you've blown it with your own kids, don't give up because you might just get another chance to do things right — with your grandkids. Not only do we have ten wonderful grandchildren — Jesse, Aaron, Adam, Rebecca, Josh, Jacob, Brent, Adama, Zackery, and Alissa, we have three great-granddaughters now: Jarah, Harley, and Peyton!

You've heard of the TV show, *How I Met Your Mother*; well this is "How I Met my Daughter-in-Law." On a hill above the boatyard where I'd moved the "Sarah Ann" was a white stucco church with "Praise the Lord" painted in large black letters. It faced the harbor where several thousand private boats and yachts were anchored and wild parties would often take place. I guess it was a reminder to people to watch their step.

One day I was checking out a classic old wooden schooner in its slip. The skipper was aboard and we started shooting the breeze and he told me that he was restoring it. He said that he was taking her out on Sunday and I was welcome to come along. I asked if I could bring along my son Jeff and he said that was fine as long as we brought our own beer. Jeff was very excited and asked if he could bring along the girl he was dating, Sandy. Even though I'd never met her, I said sure. We met at the slip, I introduced her to the others and we headed out the Corona del Mar jetty. It wasn't a great sailing, no wind. We got about five miles out when the skipper announced to everyone aboard that we had to disrobe or pick up trash from the entire boat. Jeff and I didn't want to do garbage details, so we complied, but Sandy had no interest and retired to the fantail where she sat talking with another woman, also fully dressed. She must have wondered what kind of family she was getting involved with. Other boats began to sail by and saw those of us who were nude and began waving and cheering. Some even tied up and joined in! Needless to say, the party was a success. I told you sailing was fun! All this nudity in my story; do you think there's a pattern?

By the way, Jeff and Sandy have now been married for thirty-two years and have three great sons. I sailed my own boat for fourteen years and there are many war stories I could tell, but I'll leave those for the R-rated sequel. Besides I don't want to get clobbered with a golf club like Tiger Woods did — I don't have his kind of bailout money!

Our grandson Jesse is thirty-two-years-old, and three or four years ago, he came to me and said, "Grandpa, I'd like you to marry me and my girlfriend."

I said, "What? I don't know anything about marrying people. I'm not a rabbi or a minister."

He said, "I'll check it out online." He found out that in California you can go down to the county clerk's office and get a commissioner of marriage license for one day.

I said, "Okay." The wedding was held at a classic old hotel built back in 1900 in Pasadena, the ceremony outside on a lawn and the reception inside. So I performed the ceremony. Jesse was a tall skinny kid and he and his brothers Aaron and Adam all dressed up in skinny pants and looked like the Beatles. When I was in London on one of my high school tours, I met a tailor named Friedman who had a shop on the West End; made me a sharkskin dark blue Beatles suit. I wore that suit and it fit just right! The bride's father had her dress shipped in from Italy; obviously money was no object. When I found out they were going to Europe for their honeymoon and they were going to Italy — I joked that when they stopped in Florence, they could return the gown to the rental place. I think the marriage lasted a year and-a-half before they decided to separate, although they are still good friends.

In Christmas of 2007 our granddaughter Rebecca was getting married and all the bridal party wear was rented from Men's Wearhouse. I went down there and ended up buying my tux because I thought, *Hell, I may need it for the Emmys or something; you never know.* When the fire came through, I made sure I grabbed my tux because I knew her wedding was coming. The ceremony was a civil ceremony and I used quotes from different sources and one was from Corinthians. I was performing the ceremony and I started repeating this quote when I heard my son-in-law's Jewish uncles say, "What kind of rabbi is this, quoting from Corinthians?!"

The most important thing when dealing with children, whether they are your kids or grandkids, is to always let them know how important they are to you. When they get angry with you or act belligerent, just hug them and hold them and say, "I love you." I know it's very difficult to do, but try it and you'll be surprised. What if you found out your son or daughter was gay? Would you still support his or her lifestyle and give your unconditional love? For many parents this is difficult to accept. When my children were growing up in the '50s or '60s I might have had a problem with this, but I've grown to be much more accepting of people and different lifestyles. Most of the people I know my age have become more closed-minded and become more conservative. I've gone the other direction. I think you have to keep learning and growing mentally no matter how old you get.

Your family and your kids are the most important things in life. And when you're really lucky, your wife and your sister will become best friends.

Chapter Thirty-Two

My wife Shirley and my sister Edie are more like sisters than in-laws. They met when Shirley was eighteen and Edie was ten and hit it off immediately. Shirley is the only sister Edie has. They are still very close and talk frequently over the phone even though Edie lives in Wilmington, North Carolina. She didn't go to college, she married a guy from Brooklyn who was in the printing business, and worked for the *New York Post*. She had two children, a son and a daughter. I talk to my sister all the time. Shirley and Edie both share a similar sense of humor and laugh at almost any incident no matter how small because they visualize an entire scenario in their heads.

In 1967 Edie and her family came to visit us from their then-home in Brooklyn. Edie's husband, Murray, had an aunt who lived in L.A. somewhere, so he called her up to say hello and she invited us all to dinner. Edie, Murray, and I showed up at her house.

"Where's the rest of your family?" Murray's aunt asked, "They're all invited."

I said, "Are you sure? They're quite a few."

She said, "Yes." I called Shirley and then asked Harry, my bizarre drinking friend from England, to bring Shirley, her mother visiting from Des Moines, and the three younger girls. With the aunt and her daughter, that made twelve people.

We sat around the dining room table and after a while Murray's aunt said, "Artie, will you carve the chicken? It's in the kitchen."

"Sure thing," I said. I went into the kitchen and for the first time saw the bird. It wasn't much bigger than a squab or a Cornish game hen, but if she called it a chicken, I guess it was a chicken. I cut up into very small pieces so everyone could at least have a smell, if not a taste. I think she served little round potatoes and green beans with the very, very small bits of chicken. Shirley and Edie lost it. They did their best to control their laughing and control their bladders with the embarrassment. After dinner the aunt brought out a very small pie for the twelve of us.

When we got up at the end of the evening, Murray's aunt asked, "Did everyone get enough?"

Edie chimed in, "We're stuffed!" Later Edie told me I deserved an Academy Award when I brought out that chicken platter and kept a straight face. We drove straight to Canter's Deli in the Fairfax District and ate dinner.

In July of 1990 Edie, Murray, and their daughter April, who was eighteen at the time, came out to my daughter Cindy's wedding. After the ceremony, Edie said she wanted to visit Rodeo Drive in Beverly Hills to see how the other half lived. So we went down to where all the exclusive stores are and I parked the car so we could walk Rodeo Drive. We came to a traffic light and a "don't walk" sign flashed. Two women stepped off the curb and crossed anyway. Shirley and Edie followed them and had to dodge a few cars while April waited for the walk sign.

I got really angry and yelled at them across the street, "What the hell are you thinking?"

They said, "The other women crossed!"

I yelled back, "Are you lemmings or a bunch of sheep that follow blindly?" Well, they both visualized a bunch of sheep going over a cliff and started to laugh and pee their pants. They both had on white pants, so it was pretty obvious what was happening. We walked a few blocks looking for a reasonable clothing store to buy pants and panties. Not possible on Rodeo Drive! We all walked back to the car while Edie and Shirley tried to hide their crotches. We drove to the Robinson's/May Company department store on Wilshire and Fairfax so they could buy new outfits.

Another instance was funny and sad all at the same time. In June of 1975, after spending two years in a convalescent home, my mother died. She was in and out of senility most of her time there. My sister Edie flew out from Brooklyn for the funeral. My older brother, faculty members from Lincoln and Fountain Valley schools, also attended. She is interred at Pacific View Cemetery in Corona del Mar in the Jewish section. For the service, they had set up metal folding chairs near the gravesite. The gravesite was on a very steep slope, and the chairs were arranged up and down the slope. I remember having to place my left foot down on the slope to keep myself from sliding out of the chair. Shirley and Edie were down the slope at the end of the row. After the ceremony, prayers and eulogy, people came over to offer their condolences. The vice-principal from Lincoln came through the line and when he came to me, he bent over to hug me. In his shirt pocket, he had several pens. When he straightened up, one of the pens caught me in the nose and as I stood I cried out. Shirley and Edie saw this happen and broke out in hysterical laughter, trying to muffle it as much as possible (to no avail). They both stood and turned away from the rest of us so we couldn't see their faces. Another set of wet panties! When we got back to the house, we all sat around and told our favorite stories about how Mama made us laugh. We remembered how she was before she became senile and shared many wonderful memories.

Chapter Thirty-Three

We'd decided to rebuild on the same lot, despite the risk of fires in the future. The forest service had a deal where if you hired competent people to cut and clear around your house, they would pay 75 percent of the cost. I took advantage of that and had the whole lot cleaned out. It didn't save my cedar trees or most of the pines, but it did save my oaks. We are one of the few houses that still have original oak trees.

We took the plans of the first house and expanded them so we could get more house and change all the things that we didn't like. I told Ron we needed the kitchen and dining room a little bigger. The master bedroom is much larger and has a master bathroom, walk-in closet, and two sitting areas. The new house is much more elaborate than the original. We put in all solid knotty alder doors, wild walnut hardwood flooring, tiled all the bathrooms, and built a whole suite with an added bathroom for our daughter Rochelle. Ron raised the house two feet higher above the ground, which gives us more room underneath and makes the build-up against the side of the mountain better. We had just under 2400 square feet, now we have 3400 square feet. The new house has over two hundred yards of concrete; the first had sixty. In front we built a beautiful planter with stone pillars. We went with solar electricity, solar hot water, flash tank-less water heating units, air conditioning in the master bedroom and main floor. The bottom floor has its own furnace. We put in all granite counter tops in an all-stainless steel kitchen. We bought an extra stainless refrigerator with a freezer downstairs and another little refrigerator for any guests. We also have a complete wine cellar with a wine cooler. And it's full of wine, too!

Now here's perhaps the most important piece of advice I have to offer in the entire book: If you should lose everything in a disaster, don't let your wife and daughter go shopping, especially if your insurance is paying for the loss of contents. On one of the first shopping trips after the fire, Shirley went with two of our daughters. They went up and down the aisles, throwing things in the cart, paid for all the stuff, and brought it home.

I saw it all and asked, "What did you buy?"

Shirley replied, "I don't know!" She and Rochelle continued shopping for the entire year we lived in the rental and now we have three, four, and sometimes five of the exact same item. We have four or five spatulas, six mixing and serving bowls, two or three ladles, five whisks of different sizes. I don't know if eggs get beaten differently by different-sized whisks or if they even know the difference!

We have three knife sharpeners, and we're on our third set of kitchen knives. We have three ice cream scoops, different makes for different-sized bowls. Maybe the girls are planning on opening an ice cream parlor. It's been two years since the fire, and they just bought their third set of pots and pans. The first set was made out of aluminum, and the new house has an electric induction range and can't use any pots and pans that aren't made with ferrous material. My electrician gave me a hundred bucks for that set. Then they bought Emeril Lagrasse's cookware. It worked fine except they're hard to clean. Now we're back to basics with special steel bottoms and pan sides and non-stick aluminum tops. We have two food processors, only one blender, and two coffee pots. We have several vegetable peelers; one has three blades for different surfaces and still has the tags on it. We have two sets of everyday dishes and one set of china. We end up using both sets of everyday dishes at the same time and of course, they're mismatched. The china is still in the hutch cabinet and hasn't been used. It's almost the same story with the silverware. The first set is plain, the second set has pinecones on the handles, which we never use, and the third set is still wrapped up in the hutch. We also have four bottle openers. I'm the only who drinks a beer occasionally, and corn trays and corn handles for corn on the cob ... well, I've quit counting.

To save driving time and gas money, we started ordering from catalogs. Once you start that process, you're in big trouble. All the companies that you order from sell your name and address to other companies. Here it is two years later and we're still ordering from catalogs and we get fifty catalogs in the mail every week, no exaggeration. We became so popular they come in hardcover now like encyclopedias.

We can mix, blend, stir, chop, peel, mash, fry, bake, broil, cook, boil, poach, barbecue, slice and dice, and still eat out or order take out. My kids and grandkids are reaping the benefits from excess kitchenware. It's great for them to get all this state-of-the-art kitchenware and equipment that hasn't been used for much cooking.

I don't know if people remember the film *Field of Dreams,* but the theme of the whole film was "build it and they will come." My wife has a similar philosophy which is, "spend it and it will come." That's the way we live.

In fairness, I must admit to my weakness — we have seven TVs of various sizes. I do have my wine cellar, which is my pride and joy, even though I'm not someone you would describe as a heavy drinker. Back in college I hung out a lot with a friend Al Feldman. We drank a lot of beer, listened to a lot of opera and classical music. I learned a lot about music with him and he liked a good glass of wine. I guess that was my start in enjoying red wine.

In Huntington Beach I bought a little rack for about forty bottles of wine. I stuck it inside this deep closet down on the main floor. When we moved up to the mountains, I brought that rack with me. One day I thought, *this little section of the house down by the build-up where dirt is ... I'll put in a floor and build a little wine cellar.* I bought a cheap air conditioner which wasn't really that great for wine, built the wall, and had someone come over and design a rack. When we rebuilt, the configuration of the concrete walls right at the headwall underneath the garage was so conducive for a wine cellar, with concrete walls around, I only had to put in two wooden walls and have a great cellar.

When the house was finished, the builder said, "Art, that wine cellar was free; I didn't charge you for it at all." That was another added bonus! There was some leftover insurance money from the contents of the first house that we didn't replace like the samovar and our Hummel collection, so we took that money and filled up the wine cellar. I just love sitting there and looking at all those bottles.

I started drinking at an early age probably because at all Jewish holidays, alcohol is involved. But I don't remember people getting drunk; Jews tend to overeat rather than become alcoholics. In high school there was some drinking occasionally, and at the resort I'd have a beer when we had a hot dog roast for the guests. In the service, of course we'd always head to the PX for a quick drink with the boys and then in college we'd have beer busts. After Shirley and I got married, we couldn't afford to drink very much except for beer once in a while. Then there was an English guy who hired Shirley to do some typing for him. He turned out to be a real weirdo. We decided to try to find out what was the best gin for martinis. We never did decide, but we drank a lot of martinis! After a while, he'd come over to our house every night and mix martinis. After a martini and wine with dinner I would pass out by eight o'clock. I finally had enough and told him to stop; no more! I decided to drink responsibly, which I still do today: one drink on Friday evening, one on Saturday evening and one on Sunday evening, usually a gin and tonic or a single malt scotch. I usually have wine with dinner, but I now have a built-in device that keeps me from drinking too much — I fall asleep before I can get drunk.

I really didn't take up smoking until I was in the service; I learned how to inhale on cigars. Later I switched to cigarettes and quit when I was twenty-one. I got up one morning and didn't like the taste in my mouth or the feeling in my lungs when I would try to breathe too deeply. I had half a pack in my pocket and asked one of my frat brothers if he wanted them and I quit. I did switch to pipes and cigars, but true pipe and cigar smokers don't inhale. After I moved to California I settled into the same routine I did with drinking; I only smoked Friday, Saturday, and Sunday after dinner. My kids would walk into the living room, into this haze of smoke, and make comments. I finally decided they were inhaling more smoke than I was and I quit altogether. I had about forty really great pipes, good quality, that I had in storage in the build-up of my house until the fire. I still on occasion will smoke a really good cigar, like maybe once a year. But if you don't want your kids to smoke, the best thing you can do is to stop yourself.

Chapter Thirty-Four

If I've learned anything in eighty years, it's to not let the little things get you down and always take time to enjoy the simple pleasures that surround you every day. That doesn't mean I don't have things that bug the hell out of me. So, in no particular order:

People who don't return phone calls on important business.

Repair people who call or show up and they've ordered the wrong parts. You take your car in and they don't fix what you took it in there for, especially when you're on a trip five hundred miles from the dealership.

People who don't keep their word. I believe my word is very vital to my reputation.

Students who are rude to each other and the teacher and show no respect.

Litterbugs.

Discussions with people who don't have a clue about important things like current events, economics, and politics and get their information from people like Rush Limbaugh, Glenn Beck, and Ann Coulter. They should read people like Tom Friedman and Bob Woodward and Richard Clark.

Religious zealots trying to convert me. They don't even know that Jesus and his followers were preaching Judaism. How do they know exactly where they're going after they die? They tell me I'm going to hell because I don't believe as they do. Thank God, I'm not going with them! My favorite quote is, "I would love to engage in mental combat with you, but I never do battle with an unarmed person."

People who have GPS systems and rely on them 100 percent. I recently read about a guy who drove into a lake because the GPS told him to. I read about a woman from Vegas who went to Death Valley in the middle of the summer, following her GPS. She got lost in the desert, buried the car up to it axles in sand, and her eleven-year-old son died of dehydration. Get a map and know where you're going!

How many times have you read about people using charcoal barbecues to stay warm inside their houses and they die from carbon monoxide poisoning? And how about the guy who started his car in the garage with the door closed in severe winter weather in Santa Ana, California? The furnace was on in the garage and the carbon monoxide pumped into the house and he almost killed his whole family. There is another famous quotation from Einstein; "Only two things are infinite: The universe and the stupidity of humanity, and I'm not too sure about the former."

Reality shows. *Dancing with the Stars* and all the other talent shows are fine, but many reality shows are manipulated and there's very little reality left. *Survivor, Big Brother, The Real Housewives of New Jersey, Biggest Loser, Jon and Kate Plus Eight,* and now coming up: *Octomom!* Who watches these shows?! Why do we enjoy watching other people in misery? There should be more positive TV … and forget *Wipeout,* an obstacle course that's impossible!

If you listen to the news first thing in the morning, you hear, "Breaking news; there's a wind advisory and high surf coming in. Stay away from western-facing beaches and jetties!" And then on the nightly news you hear, "Breaking news again; people drown while standing on the jetty in San Pedro." Don't these people understand how dangerous it is? What is the matter with them?

People who don't know what they are doing. When I was sailing, there were three courses from the Coast Guard where you learn all the basics about anchoring, safely filling your power boat with gasoline, and other important items. If you anchor your boat, you're supposed to have at least three times as much chain as the depth of the water. Or if you were chain and line, seven times anchor line as depth of the water. I can't tell you how many times I sailed to Catalina, where the water off the casino is eighty to ninety feet deep, and some guy would come along and drop his anchor so it would just touch the bottom. He'd get off the boat, go onshore, come back and his boat would be gone floating off about a half-mile out at sea. People wouldn't take classes to learn the basics about sailing a boat. They would go fill their boats with gasoline, not realizing that gasoline vapors are heavier than the air. It's basic information given freely from Coast Guard courses and books. People would fill up, leave the companionway open, and the gasoline vapors would go down into the bilge. They'd put the pump back on the dock, get in, and start up their engine and blow up their boat! The spark from the engine would ignite the vapors.

Man's inhumanity to man. Why are we so inhumane to each other, brutal, vicious, and murderous? I know you've heard it before, but we're the only animal species that acts this way. Religions of the world seem to promote it rather than deter it, especially the fanatic fringe who thinks, "Believe as we do, or you're doomed."

I can't help mention something about politics. I admit I'm a Democrat, but I've voted for Republicans when I agreed with their philosophy. But the Republican party has taken such an extreme right position, it not only wants nothing to change, it seems to want to go backward. Republicans have taken words like "socialism" and "liberalism" and made them dirty words. Social Security, Medicare, and unemployment insurance are examples of socialism that seem to work. Liberalism. Our forefathers who broke away from Great Britain — Washington, John Adams, Jefferson, Ben Franklin — were the liberals in that conflict. The Constitution, the Bill of Rights, the thirteenth, fourteenth, and fifteenth amendments, social security, the women's right to vote, the reforms of the 1930s, civil rights legislation were all "liberal" ideas that have become a part of mainstream America. Not all liberal ideas should be enacted, but not all liberal ideas are bad. The current Republican party is NOT the party of Barry Goldwater and Everett Dirksen or even Richard Nixon. Under Nixon the EPA was passed; he opened the door to China. Some Republicans and extreme right-wing media are bent on seeing President Obama fail, no matter what his proposals are. These people are not patriotic or love America. I love this country and I don't care who's in office as long as he does what he truly feels is best for the country.

Greed. When I read the Bernie Madoff story of how he scammed billions of dollars from all those people, it made me sick. He stole from his own people. He became the poster boy for anti-Semitism. There are many more greedy CEOs and scam artists out there; he's just one of the most successful.

Evolution. There are people who believe dinosaurs were on Noah's ark and the earth is no more than 6000 years old. Where are these dinosaurs now? Where did Noah get all the animals from South and North America and Australia that didn't exist in the Middle East? The Jews wrote the story of creation and I've yet to meet one who accepts the Old Testament literally. I imagine the ultra-orthodox do, but they are in a small minority.

Don't ever forget that doctors are just human beings. In the summer of 2009, Shirley and I had an appointment with her gastroenterologist so he could perform an endoscope of her stomach and the upper section of her small intestine. When the nurse reviewed her drug regimen, Shirley advised her that she was taking both Plavix and regular doses of aspirin. The doctor then proceeded to perform the procedure and took thirteen biopsies. That evening at home, she started to throw up blood. I called the doctor and he said if she did it again to take her to the local emergency room. She continued so I rushed her to the emergency room. Although they treated her, they weren't equipped to deal with the seriousness of her condition so they rushed her by ambulance over twenty miles down the hill to San Bernardino Hospital intensive care. The doctor there immediately did another endoscope (without anesthetic because she couldn't handle it) and injected each biopsy with epinephrine to stop the bleeding. During her three days in intensive care, and five more in a regular room, she was given eight units of blood and plasma, which is the total amount of blood in the body of an average woman. Although the original doctor was competent and reliable, do you think if he knew his patient better and realized she was such a bleeder he would have proceeded differently? He told us doing an endoscope on a patient taking Plavix and aspirin was common, but in this case it was nearly fatal. You must be responsible for your own health. Doctors are so busy today, and their heads are so filled with technical information that they have lost touch with the patient. You must be your advocate when it comes to your health, and don't just blindly trust the doctor without making sure he or she knows the specifics of your case.

Education. The United States remains the greatest economic and military power in the world, but can we stay there? In order to compete in all fields, we must have the finest education system. Presently that is not the case. We need to be training our young people in science, engineering, and mathematics. In many European countries, as well as in Japan, India, and China, government leaders come from these fields. In the United States, almost all of our leaders are lawyers. We have to make changes or we might end up only leading the world in suing each other.

Terrorism. I don't know how we're going to stop it because it's very difficult to deal with fanatics who are willing to commit suicide to achieve their goals. Some of you may object to me saying so, but I believe that any religious fanatic whether Jewish, Christian, or Muslim is not healthy for creating peace. All major religions claim that there's only one God; why don't we have one religion? In my opinion, we're fighting over semantics.

Global warming. Scientists say that half of global warming is caused by forgotten gases like methane, not just CO2. Although CO2 from fossil fuels is obviously a major problem, methane is produced by landfills and other decomposing organic materials — not to mention emissions from cattle and humans! So what do we do with this gas? Collect it and use it for power? Put a catalytic converter on all those rectal orifices? Feed all these people and animals Gas-X? The next time you fart think about this — there were 1.3 billion humans in 1900, 6.8 billion now. Do you think all that gas had something to do with global warming?

I can't move on without mentioning the disastrous eight years of George W. Bush. I think his administration will go down in history as one of the worst, if not the worst, America has ever elected. President Bush represented the conservative wing of the Republican party. The conservatives consider themselves the guardians of the constitution, yet Bush and his administration did more to violate the constitution with the Patriot Act and all the other regulations he got passed than any other president in my lifetime. Of course, I think FDR allowing the Japanese-American internment camps during World War II was a violation of the constitution. The Bush administration did all sorts of searches without warrants, suspended the writ of habeas corpus, used tortuous interrogation methods in Iraq, Guantanamo, and in secret foreign prisons. With all that happened, the Iraqi War was being planned before 9/11. We had 50,000 troops in Kuwait before 9/11 training for the invasion. Saddam Hussein could have been captured and removed a helluva lot easier and helluva lot cheaper with a lot of lives saved. We lost over 4,000 troops and an estimated 100,000 or more Iraqi civilians. Read Richard Clarke's books, *Against all Enemies* and *Your Government Failed You.* Clarke served as a CIA expert and an advisor. Bush ran the country with decisions made from his gut. I have a gut feeling that his cronies Karl Rove, Dick Cheney, Paul Wolfowitz, and Donald Rumsfeld would support what his gut was feeling or what his gut was thinking. He probably thought with his gut because he had insufficient brain power or it was overloaded.

His first cabinet pick was Secretary of State Colin Powell, which I thought was a great choice. But then Bush gave him a bunch of false, misleading information about weapons of mass destruction and sent him to the UN to make a case for invading Iraq. Bush instilled fear, not only in the U.S., but in the rest of the world. He made his case for war and Congress gave him permission. Whatever happened to the stipulation in the Constitution that states only Congress can declare war, which they haven't used since World War II?

Paul O'Neill was Bush's Secretary of the Treasury. Formerly the president of Alcoa Aluminum, O'Neill and his friend Alan Greenspan, chairman of the Federal Reserve Board at the time, had a plan to improve Social Security with help from the surplus that President Clinton left when his term ended. Secretary O'Neill presented the plan to President Bush at a cabinet meeting. President Bush looked at him for a moment and then said, "No, I'll just present what I said on the campaign trail." Bush only wanted cabinet members who would rubberstamp his views. Did you also notice O'Neill missing from the cabinet after that? I also read Paul O'Neill's book. All the corruption and illegalities and secrecy have yet to be exposed. At the beginning of Bush's first term, there was a big secret meeting about energy policy. Why should our energy policy be a secret? What was the plan, who was there, and what was secret? The business of the White House was kept secret. Why? I thought this was <u>our</u> country. The presidency should be transparent, unless it involves national security. You could write volumes about Bush's mess. He probably set the country back twenty years or more in some areas. Just think of how our history would have been different had Gore been elected, which was later proven that he was!

This is aimed at all people in government. Originally our forefathers designed the government so that all people elected went to Washington, D.C. to serve the country, not to make careers and enrich themselves while their community waits. One of the biggest problems our country has is that almost everybody spends most of their time, effort, and money working toward getting re-elected rather than doing the job they were sent there to do. Although lobbyists are legal, they contribute to this situation. Most people have never heard of James K. Polk, the eleventh president of the U.S. Some historians consider him to be the most successful president in American history. He made four campaign promises: to lower tariffs, settle the dispute with Texas, settle or pay for the Mexican Territory, and negotiate and pay for the Oregon Territory. He kept all four promises, served one term in office and left. By the way, he also had his gall bladder removed when he was seventeen-years-old using only brandy as an anesthetic. Why can't we have more people in the government like him?

I was thinking maybe we should forgive President Bush for the miserable job he did. He wasn't really that bright; he bit off more than he could chew; he was way in over his head. The job overwhelmed him. His father probably talked him into it because his brother Jeb didn't want to run. The fault really lies with the American people for allowing the country to have a president like him for eight years. The first election was stolen by Bush. He got involved in the Iraq War through lies and deception. You would think that the people would have learned, but NOOOOOOO. They elected him for another term. The problem lies with the apathy of the American public. The twenty-sixth amendment was passed to give eighteen-year-olds the right to vote, and yet they have the worst voting record of any age group. In presidential elections, the percentage of eligible voters who turn out is somewhere in the 50 percent range. In Australia, 98 percent of the people vote. I have to tell you, it's illegal not to vote in Australia. I don't know if that's a good idea or not. You've heard the old saying, "Bad things happen when good people do nothing." Well at least we have President Obama. It seems he wants to take the country in a new, better direction, but we'll have to wait and see.

Of course, we still have Sarah Palin traipsing all over the country with the "tea-baggers," criticizing the Obama administration on every level. I've yet to hear her come up with any positive, constructive plans to solve our current problems. She seems to be vying for the 2012 Republican nomination. Some people believe the Mayan calendar which says the world will end in the year 2012. Do you think Sarah Palin is one of the indicators? Can't the Republican party find a qualified candidate to run for the presidency? There are still conservatives claiming that Obama isn't a U.S. citizen. His mother was a U.S. citizen and he was born in Hawaii; don't they know Hawaii became a state in 1950? Bill Maher has said that he will produce Obama's birth certificate when Sarah Palin produces her high school diploma. Isn't that funny? Well, I thought it was! If you want to know the truth about George W. Bush read *American Dynasty* by Kevin Phillips, *The Price of Loyalty* by Ron Suskind, and *What Happened* by Scott McClellan. McClellan had known Bush most of his life, worked for him in Texas, and became his press secretary. O'Neill was part of Bush's cabinet and Phillips is a very reputable author. None of these people have an axe to grind or anything to gain by publishing these books.

I guess that's enough negativity. I'm really a very positive person and there are a lot more things to love about this country than to dislike. I just want the U.S. to be the best and stay on top. Being a former teacher, unnecessary stupidity just bugs me. Besides, focusing on negative things only makes you a negative person. Life has much more rewarding things to offer.

Here are some books I recommend if you want to read more about these subjects, and to prove to you I'm not just making this stuff up off the top of my head:

The Baby Thief by Barbara Bisantz Raymond
Man's Search for Meaning by Viktor Frankl
What Happened by Scott McClellan
The Assault on Reason by Al Gore
The Betrayal of America by Vincent Bugliosi
Hot, Flat and Crowded by Tom Friedman
The War Within by Bob Woodward
Bush at War by Bob Woodward
Reinventing the Body, Resurrecting the Soul by Deepak Chopra
Against all Enemies by Richard Clarke
Your Government Failed You Richard Clarke
American Dynasty by Kevin Phillips
The Price of Loyalty by Ron Suskind

Chapter Thirty-Five

I like to think about the little things in life, the small pleasures that make you happy. Making love to a beautiful woman; if you're married, hopefully it's your wife. There are many other things that make me smile: The smell of a beautiful rose or gardenia; newly-mown hay; the sight of a bright starry night in the desert or out in the country where there are no city lights; watching a crackling fire in your pot-bellied stove or fireplace on a snowy winter night. A cool summer evening in New England sitting on the lawn listening to the crickets and other sounds of the night, maybe owls. Seeing the fireflies come out. Or how about the taste of a fine wine or a really good cognac? Standing on top of Mount Whitney and checking out the view; it could be a hundred or more miles. Out sailing in forty or fifty knot winds with the rail buried and the spray coming over the bow. Scuba diving through kelp beds and checking out the sea life. Maybe some of you like a good ski run down the mountain or flying a small plane over the Grand Canyon or some other scenic spot. Sitting in your wine cellar and checking out your fifty cases of wine — maybe that's not such a small pleasure.

There's so much unhappiness in our country and probably others because people do not enjoy what they do to make a living. Even though they make large amounts of money, some people are unhappy because they have to go to work everyday. Work should not be considered work. When you go to your job you should be there because you love doing what you're doing — you're happy, you're helping other people, you're putting something forth that you can leave behind you for the next generation — you're doing something worthwhile. If you don't feel that you're doing something worthwhile, then you should go get retrained and find another job that you enjoy. Life's too short. I don't know where people think we came from, or who created us, but whatever you think, whatever your religion may be — life is so precious it should not be wasted on something that you hate to do. You should be happy. What makes you happy makes everyone around you happy. No one wants to be around someone who's bitching and complaining about what they have to do every day to make a living.

I'm no philosopher but in over eighty years on the planet I've made my share of mistakes and learned plenty of lessons. From my experience, here are some insights I can guarantee you will make you happier and enrich your life:

1. Cherish your family — my wife and my kids are my closest friends.
2. Don't marry someone to make you happy. You have to love yourself first and be happy with yourself before you can share your love with someone else.
3. Don't become obsessed with your goals or getting rich; live life as it comes along.
4. Don't regret the things you could have done but didn't.
5. The value system in the U.S. is really screwed up. You always hear politicians and government leaders speak about the future and how our children are one of our greatest assets, yet for the most part the public school system in this country is pathetic and getting worse.
6. Marriage is hard work. There are so many things you have to change about yourself, many compromises, much give and take. If you're open to your partner, there is so much to learn from each other. The end result, the rewards far outweigh the effort you put in, especially if you picked the right person. I was very lucky, because I certainly did.

So here I am sitting on my back deck of my brand new home, looking at a beautiful view of the forest and Mount San Gorgonio, 11,499 feet, the tallest mountain in southern California. Being a retired history and geography teacher, I can't help myself, I have to mention the details. Does it sound like I'm bragging? I probably am, but I'm so elated about where I am in my life, I can't contain myself. Usually by the time you're in your sixties, where you are is where you stay the rest of your life. Well, you don't have to, and I didn't. If you're mentally alert and physically fit and keep active in both of those areas, you'll stay that way. Where does it say that as you age, you have to stop doing nearly everything and become a couch potato?

As I write this a new year has begun, I celebrated my eighty-second birthday and my soulmate wife and I celebrated our sixtieth wedding anniversary. I feel like we're closer now than we've ever been. Most of the things I've done in my life have turned out positively. I did not give a great deal of thought to any of my decisions. The few stumbles I had along the way turned out to be unimportant or insignificant when considering the big picture. Did I live a charmed life, was it divine intervention, naïve fearlessness or just plain luck? Maybe it was all because of my positive attitude — or maybe all of the above. In his book, *Reinventing the Body, Resurrecting the Soul,* Deepak Chopra says that if you think you've lived a charmed life it means you're in touch with your soul. I feel like I've always been positive, had a great outlook, and didn't dwell on the negative. I had many people tell me about bad experiences they had in Europe, yet when I was there I couldn't figure out what they were talking about. I think if you treat people well, they will respond in kind.

I don't have a definitive answer about my life's journey. You can receive all the good advice in the world, but you still have to figure out how to live your life yourself. The nicest thing anyone can say about you is that you are a real mensch — it's a Yiddish word. In a nutshell, a person is a mensch because he or she simply does the right thing and makes others feel good about themselves. A mensch is an upright, honorable, decent person — someone to admire and emulate, someone of noble character. Everyone should strive toward this. I'm still working on it.

Well, it's that time of day to go down to my wine cellar, get a good bottle, pour myself a glass, look out at the mountains, and watch the changing colors of the snow as the sun sets in the west. I have to start thinking about my next project or career change. Maybe a screenplay about my life and then produce a movie. I'm almost there but not done yet! As my mother would say, "Auf Wiedersehen, geh gesunde heit hachen ein guten schlet weg!"

Los Angeles Times

Wednesday September 18, 1996

Stolen Identity
*Shirley Frankel of Huntington Beach has searched for her birth family for 30 years. Though the discovery that her adoption records were fabricated makes success seemingly impossible, she's not willing to give up.

Orange County Edition, Life & Style, Page E-1
View Desk
44 inches; 1569 words
Type of Material: Profile

By DEBRA CANO, SPECIAL TO THE TIMES
For most of her life, Shirley Frankel has wondered over and over: "Who am I?"

Sometime before Frankel was placed with her adoptive family when she was about 6 months old, she was given a false identity--one so completely fabricated that she will probably never find the answer to the question that haunts her.

"I have no history," says Frankel, 65, of Huntington Beach. "I don't know if I was stolen. I don't know my genetic background or why I'm allergic to wheat. . . . This is my whole life," she says as she waves her bogus adoption records, part of the paper trail in a frustrating 30-year search to find her birth parents.

Frankel's adoption was one of many handled by Georgia Tann, now infamous for making a fortune black-marketing babies when she headed the Tennessee Children's Home Society in Memphis.

Her birth records had not simply been altered but represented a stolen identity. The same birth certificate, birth date and same mother and father belonged to someone else--someone completely unrelated.

When Frankel learned what had happened, she cried for days.

"I was so discouraged," she says. "All the times before, I would hit dead-ends. But this time it was a brick wall."

Each year, thousands of adoptees in this country search for their birth families. According the California Adoption Alliance, the best guess of the search and reunification movement is that between 2% and 4% of all adoptees search each year. The majority is successful--except in cases where records were falsified, as in Frankel's case.

Attitudes about adoption have changed so dramatically that today not only do adoptees and birth parents establish contact if they wish, but a birth mother often chooses the family where her child will be placed.

Frankel's case stands in stark contrast.

Not only was there deception in the original arrangements, but Frankel's adoptive mother never discussed the adoption with her--it was off-limits as a topic of conversation.

*

Frankel and her husband, Art, who have been married 46 years, have five children and nine grandchildren. She is a document processor for an insurance brokerage firm; he is a retired high school counselor and teacher.

The fullness of Frankel's life has not erased her longing to feel connected to an ancestry.

It was March 1932 when she was adopted by George and Libbie Marsh, Russian Jewish immigrants who lived in Des Moines.

Her adoptive father owned a taxi and rental car business, and her adoptive mother was a housewife. Both were 41.

Because of their ages and desire to adopt a Jewish child, Frankel said, it was probably difficult for them to adopt in their home state. The Marshes had contacted their rabbi, who knew of another Des Moines couple who had adopted a Jewish child through the Children's Home Society in Memphis.

At the time of Frankel's adoption in 1932, the Memphis branch was run by Tann, who in 1950 was accused of selling babies and reportedly made at least $1 million handing over infants to adoptive parents who believed she was dealing honestly with them. It is estimated that from the early 1920s to 1950, about 5,000 children were adopted through the Memphis branch, though not all were illegally surrendered or placed. As the case broke, Tann died of cancer, taking with her the truth about what transpired in Frankel's adoption and that of many others.

Frankel now doubts that she is from a Jewish background, as Tann purported in arranging the adoption.

"I probably was a Southern Baptist, if anything," says Frankel, who was raised in the Jewish Orthodox traditions and learned to speak Yiddish from her adoptive grandmother.

Frankel figures that even the Sept. 9 birth date she has called her own for so many years is not accurate.

*

As a child, Frankel says, she was teased by neighborhood children who told her the Marshes were not her natural mother and father.

"I confronted my mother, and she told me, 'It doesn't make any difference. You're like my own flesh and blood.' She said she loved me as if I was her own child."

The subject was never brought up again.

"Back then, you didn't discuss things like that. My mother was very strict and rigid," Frankel says.

When Frankel was nearly 6, her adoptive father died. Her mother supported them by sewing for the military, then working in alterations at a department store in Des Moines.

Frankel was about 11 when her curiosity about her adoption was again fueled. She had discovered a leather accordion file in her mother's bedroom dresser that contained adoption papers naming Hazel Beal as an unwed Memphis woman who had given birth to a daughter named "Sarah."

"I knew it was me, but I was too young to realize what adoption actually meant," Frankel says.

Throughout her childhood, there were many times when Frankel would sneak into the bedroom and peek at the adoption papers.

When Frankel met her future husband at a college fraternity party in Des Moines in 1948, she was 16 and still in high school.

"Shirley was ashamed to tell me she was adopted," says Art Frankel, who was 20 and a student at Drake University in Des Moines when they met. "Her mother made it a shameful thing."

Libbie Marsh died in 1971 from cancer without ever discussing the adoption with her daughter.

Even as Frankel had children of her own, her questions about her past persisted: Why was she was put up for adoption? Why was she so sickly as a newborn? Did she have any siblings? Did she inherit the intolerance to wheat gluten that is so strong she can't eat pizza, cookies, cakes--anything made with flour?

In 1967, Frankel and her husband embarked on a search for her birth mother. They had little information to go on. Only the name Hazel Beal.

Shirley Frankel had written to Tennessee's Office of Vital Statistics and the Department of Human Services for her birth certificate but was told her records were sealed. When Tann's baby-selling business was uncovered, all records were sent to Nashville.

Over the years, Frankel contacted various organizations that she hoped could help locate her family. Among them was Tennessee's The Right to Know, a nonprofit group co-founded by Denny Glad that has helped more than 1,000 adoptees search for their birth families.

Glad has assisted many adoptees, birth parents and birth siblings affected by the adoptions arranged through the Memphis Children's Home Society.

"When [Tann] charged fees, people paid in good faith, not thinking they were buying a child, and she put the money in her own pocket," Glad says.

"The power went to [Tann's] head. It was the idea that she could play God and give people children who couldn't get them any other way."

Even with the experience she acquired working on other Tann cases, Glad was unable to help Frankel.

*

Despite many dead-ends, the Frankels continued to pursue every angle they could.

When Art Frankel read a newspaper article in 1992 about the federal government releasing the 1920 Census, he started combing through records at the federal building in Laguna Niguel.

"I went through thousands of names hoping to find a Hazel Beal," Art Frankel says. "I went through all the records from Tennessee, Arkansas and Mississippi."

He found a Hazel Beal from Jackson, Tenn., who would have been old enough to give birth to a child in 1931. The Frankels contacted everyone named Beal in Jackson and neighboring cities, but no one had heard of Hazel Beal.

One of their contacts suggested they call Peggy D. Mathes, a Nashville attorney who has assisted adoptees in gaining access to their records. Tennessee laws had become more relaxed, and Mathes had success in obtaining records for others.

In May 1992, the Frankels hired Mathes to obtain a court order to open her records, and by late August, she secured the order. Within a month, Frankel had her birth certificate and many pages of documents--including her adoption file and background on the Memphis Children's Home Society.

That was when Frankel learned that her supposed birth mother, Hazel Beal, was not. Beal was married to William Cohen from Memphis, and they had a daughter--a daughter they raised--who has the same birth date as Frankel. The birth information was apparently "borrowed" to help build the false identity given Frankel. The records also showed aunts, uncles, siblings and other relatives--all of whom turned out to be fictitious.

*

"It's a real strange case. It's the only one I've ever had like this, and I've opened a lot of adoption records," says Mathes, whose cases have included 25 from the Memphis Children's Home Society. "I didn't know what to tell Mrs. Frankel. . . . I felt so sorry for her. Just the fact that she couldn't find out . . . what her origins were."

Frankel's case is also the first one Glad said she has seen since she began conducting searches 18 years ago in which the records were "totally fabricated from beginning to end."

Over the years, Glad's organization has encountered records in which information such as income, education, religion and age were false or conflicting. But more often than not, Glad says, there are some clues that help lead to a successful search.

Glad says Tann frequently falsified information to make it appear that a child had a Jewish background.

Because anti-Semitism was prevalent at the time of Frankel's birth, Glad says Jewish people found it difficult to adopt children.

"They found they could get a child through Tann, and she was very willing to oblige," she says.

Based on her study of Frankel's records, Glad speculates that Tann found herself in a dilemma when her superior from the Nashville headquarters-- rather than Tann herself--delivered Frankel to the Marshes.

"My educated guess is that Tann had no records of this child and found herself in a situation she couldn't handle and so she had to come up with a record."

*

L. Anne Babb, president of the American Adoption Congress, a Washington, D.C.-based organization that advocates access to adoption records and ethical adoption processes, says that since the mid-1970s, hundreds of thousands of adoptees nationwide have take steps to have their birth records opened or find their natural families.

"As many as 88,000 different adoptees per year are searching at any given time in the United States," Babb says, "a figure consistent with the high percentage of adoptees who want information about their origins."

Babb says she has spoken with "hundreds, perhaps thousands" of adoptees and birth mothers whose records were falsified to some extent. In some instances, expectant mothers were given an alias in a maternity home, or an adoption agency used an alias without the mother's knowledge.

Whatever form the deception takes, Babb says, "falsifying birth records is highly unethical."

*

The deception in Frankel's adoption papers continues to take its toll more than six decades later.

Her questions linger: Was she sold by Tann? Was her biological mother coerced into giving her up? Where did she live the first six months of her life before her adoption? Who are her birth parents?

Frankel and her husband know there is almost no hope she will ever find her birth relatives--a realization she says is heartbreaking.

Still, Frankel hangs on to one piece of the puzzle that has felt real to her. She drives a car with a personalized license plate bearing the name that appears on her adoption papers: "Sara."

References:

The following is a list of books that I have read while writing my biography. These books support my facts and opinions.

"Reinventing the Body, Resurrecting the Soul", by Deepak Chopra

"The World is Flat" and "Hot Flat and Crowded", by Thomas Freidman

"Assault on Reason", by Al Gore

"What Happened", by Scott McClellan

"Man's Search for Meaning", by Victor Frankl

"American Dynasty", by Kevin Phillips

"Against All Enemies", "The Government Failed You", and "Cyber War" by Richard Clarke

"Super Freak Onomics", Levitt and Dubner

"The War Within", by Bob Woodward

"Betrayal of America", by Vincent Bugliosi

"Price of Loyalty", by Paul O'Neil

"If You Can't Say Anything Nice, Say It In Yiddish", by Lita Epstein